C0-BPU-256

A THEOLOGY
OF THE
IN-BETWEEN

A THEOLOGY OF THE IN-BETWEEN

THE VALUE OF SYNCRETIC PROCESS

BY

Carl F. Starkloff

MARQUETTE
UNIVERSITY

PRESS

BR
127
.S775
2002

Marquette Studies in Theology
No. 33

Andrew Tallon, Series Editor

Library of Congress Cataloguing in Publication Data

Starkloff, Carl F., 1933-
  A theology of the in-between : the value of syncretic process / by
Carl F. Starkloff.
     p. cm. — (Marquette studies in theology ; no. 33)
Includes bibliographical references and index.
  ISBN 0-87462-685-4 (pbk. : alk. paper)
  1. Christianity and other religions. 2. Syncretism (Religion) 3.
Indians of North America—Religion. 4. Syncretism (Religion)—North
America. I. Title. II. Marquette studies in theology ; #33.
  BR127 .S775 2002
  261.2—dc21
                              2002014545

© 2002 Marquette University Press
All rights reserved.

Cover design by Andrew J. Tallon

Marquette University Press is a member of the
ASSOCIATION OF AMERICAN UNIVERSITY PRESSES

MARQUETTE UNIVERSITY PRESS
MILWAUKEE

The Association of Jesuit University Presses

Contents

Preface 7
Introduction 9

Chapter 1: *The European Epoch:*
The Metaxy Between 100 and 1300 19
The Church Fathers 22
Discerning an Authentic Process 25
Passage 33
Contact with Barbarian Tribes 37
The Rational Synthesis 45

Chapter 2: *Toward a Theology of the In-Between* 53
The Philosophy of the In-Between: An Interpretive Key
Toward a Theological Method 53
The Methodology of Bernard Lonergan 61
Transcendental Precepts 63
Conversion 64
The Role of Functional Specialties 68

Chapter 3: *Into the Context: "Syncretic Action"* 89
"Bringing in Our Culture" 90
Bricolage 94
First Context: The Sun Dance People 101
Second Context: The Peyote Movement and
Native American Church 121
Theological Analysis 126

Conclusion 139

Appendix 1: *Christian Views of Syncretism* 143
Origins of the Word As Solution Rather Than Problem ... 143
Syncretism as Unprincipled Commingling 145
Contemporary Positions: The "Power Encounter" 148
Syncretism as a Metaxic Dialogue 150

Appendix 2: *Non-Confessional Views of Syncretism* 157
Phenomenological Treatments of Syncretism 159
Antiquity 159
The Middle Ages 161
Contemporary Phenomena 162
Definitions 163

Bibliography 167

Index 175

"This is the will of God for you in Christ Jesus: do not extinguish the Spirit; do not despise prophecy; test all things and hold fast to what is good."
1 Thessalonians 5:18-21

PREFACE

Perhaps the highest merit in the following work, given its heavy analytical tone, is the fact that its origin was very much "the field." Had I not become deeply involved with spiritual leaders of the Arapaho people prior to 1981, and with the Ojibway people of northern Ontario after that time, this subject would not likely have occurred to me. But it is now clear to me how applicable the various works on syncretism are to these people, given their struggles to survive in an overwhelmingly dominant society and in a Church that is so very European.

I am grateful to have been in some small way included in that struggle, and I express here my thanks to those leaders and to all the Arapahos and Ojibways whom I have known over a period of four decades. I will not attempt to name any of them here, since it would be so easy to overlook some. I have, however, in the course of this book, mentioned by name some who were especially significant in spurring me on to further reflection and action. I can only hope that, indirectly, this book will help them and other aboriginal societies to enjoy a secure home in the Church and within the wider secular world.

Special thanks are due to my superiors at Regis College in Toronto for having granted me more leisure time for writing during my final year of full tenure there. I am happy to be able to continue serving Regis in some way as a *professor emeritus*, while now serving as adjunct faculty in the Theological Studies Department and Vice President for Mission and Ministry at St. Louis University. I also thank Dr. Andrew Tallon, the director of Marquette University Press, for his willingness to take a chance with a topic that seems to most to be so esoteric, and thus to make my ideas available to others who share my quest.

St. Louis University
2002

INTRODUCTION

In launching into such a complex topic as syncretism, I find it necessary to violate a certain canon of writing and to state what this book is not about. It is not a discussion of interfaith dialogue or pluralism, even though these issues are closely related. To state my own position on that set of issues, I hold with a recent comment of Jacques Dupuis that historical pluralism is here to stay, and that God seems not to be unhappy with it—in fact even wills it in human history. (Dupuis, 1997, 386-387). This situation will always call for open dialogue among faiths as well as constant meditation on the Christian belief in the unique mediation of Jesus Christ.

What, then, *is* the book about? It is totally concerned with the phenomenon that develops whenever a particular culture embraces or is touched deeply by a "universal religion"; it is a phenomenon that leads to questions of diversity of symbols, of beliefs, of doctrines, and of ethics. This book therefore accepts the *fact* of 2000 years of Christian mission across cultural boundaries. It also accepts mission as a valid movement, however badly it may have been carried out in so many cases. That is, if a person or community believe that something momentous—a "gospel"—has happened in their lives, they desire to share this happening with others. There may well be contexts within which evangelizing mission should not continue, such as clear signs that local people are truly happy in their own religion, or that the people very definitely inform missionaries that they are not welcome to remain. Being myself a historical "pluralist" (like Dupuis) and a theological "inclusivist," to employ those very unsatisfactory terms, I would and actually have functioned with the policy of testifying to my faith but not trying to impose it—in fact, of offering to leave if so requested. But as for those Christian theologians who condemn all forms of mission, I would have to ask: what would *they* be engaged in today if that position had been the policy from the beginning? Would they prefer to be following the religions of their various tribal ancestors?

I do not intend to argue that point here, since mission and
conversions are simply a *fact* of two millennia. My purpose in this
book is to address the question of the dynamics at work in acculturation and inculturation, that is, the inevitable mixing of elements that
occurs whenever cultures and religions meet (acculturation), and
especially when one culture adopts and appropriates a new religion
(inculturation). That is, I am concerned with what happens, not when
different religions simply co-exist, but when they mingle, when they
"syncretize." This fact makes the present book basically a missiological
one, since mission and syncretism have always been companion
phenomena. Hence, I intend this for a readership of persons concerned with mission, and especially with coming to terms, not so
much with "pluralism," but a plurality of experiences and world views
within one overarching religion.

One of the more entertaining aspects of doing research into the
subject of syncretism has been the reactions of various persons when
one mentions being involved in such a project. Laypersons (i.e. here,
non-professional theologians) simply register puzzlement and try to
show a polite curiosity through glazed-over eyes as one talks about the
subject. Students beginning a program in theology tend to grow
impatient at being kept from more relevant topics. Quite the opposite
is the case with many religious professionals such as church adminis-
trators, pastors and missionaries: to them, syncretism is what I have for
some time now called "a ten-letter four-letter word." Historian of
religions Kurt Rudolph, from his investigations of the term's usage
over the last four centuries, has dubbed it a "scolding word" *Scheltwort*
and "a theological term of abuse" (*ein theologisches Schimpfwort*)
(Rudolph, 1979,194-195). In his introduction to the World Council
of Churches' "Guidelines on Dialogue," Stanley Samartha wrote
apropos of this,

> Perhaps no other word in the ecumenical vocabulary has aroused
> more fears, created more unnecessary controversy, and, more often
> then not, succeeded in sidetracking urgent issues in the life of the
> churches in pluralist situations than the term syncretism. One
> reason for this is the negative connotation the term has acquired in
> the context of mission (Anderson and Stransky, 1981, 130).

While I do not fully embrace Samartha's pluralist position, I vigorously concur that this word is capable of triggering knee-jerk reactions. Such reactions have led some missiologists to suggest that the word should be consigned to the rubbish heap of worthless jargon. Understandably enough, J. Peter Schineller (1992) has recommended this solution, but his colleague, Robert J. Schreiter (1993), writing in a response article, believes that the problem cannot be dismissed so easily. As I hope to illustrate, I believe that syncretism is a word which, much as Karl Barth's critics once said of him, is a mountain that must be climbed rather than walked around, by all theologians of inculturation, contextualization and indigenization. In fact, extensive literary study of world-wide religious interaction throughout history, of the labors of theologians since the early centuries of Christianity, and my own "field experience" emphatically support this argument. The syncretic process (a phrase that I prefer) seems to be a dynamic built into human nature and a process of all human social and religious interaction. The syncretic process is a *de facto* human dynamism that is not going to be dismissed, however critical we may have to be in studying it. It is, in my theological opinion, "connatural" with, not the heritage of sin, but of a laudable desire of humans for unity within diversity. Consequently, the purpose of this book is not to defend syncretism as such (as an "-ism"), but to approach it as part of the never-ending historical quest for wholeness. While appreciating Diana Eck's recent comments on it in her fascinating study of pluralism (Eck, 1993, 196), and her reasons for not wishing to be "detained" by the topic, I intend to spend this entire book being detained by it. I hope that readers will allow themselves to be detained along with me.

The best beginning for this discussion, I think, is an anecdote, one not unlike those that could be narrated by many missionaries and cross-cultural workers among societies exposed fairly recently to Christianity. The reality was most vividly symbolized for me about sixteen years ago in a conversation with an old friend, a former adviser, parishioner and Arapaho elder, the late Ben Friday, Sr. This man was a devoutly practicing Roman Catholic, a political figure widely respected well beyond his tribal boundaries, and a traditional spiritual leader. Yet Ben was also a former Episcopalian who had entered the

Catholic Church through his wife's influence, and one of the "Four
Old Men" who guide the entire complex of the Arapaho "Sun Dance"
and the tribe's spiritual affairs in general. Ben, whom we shall meet
again later in this book, used to enjoy stirring the pot in religious
conversations by declaring that he practiced three religions—Catholic, Episcopalian, and Arapaho! We Catholic leaders, along with the
Episcopalian vicars on the Wind River Reservation, agreed not to
quarrel with the *credo* of this local leader, because, among other
reasons, we were unwilling to put a closure on dialogue among the
churches and among the native spiritual leaders. As to my sense of
what Ben meant, we shall study this in due order.

But there are other realities within the Christian fold that demand
that we deal with the very concept of syncretism. While anthropologists and historians of religion have been able to examine syncretism
with *relatively* detached "objectivity," leaders of the churches have
generally responded to it with horror, even if in most cases they have
never seriously studied its meaning; it is simply taken to be synony-
mous with heresy. The word seems to have become a kind of shibbo-
leth that *ipso facto* admits one to a particular theological camp. Most
commonly, among evangelical Protestants, it seems to be equated
with idolatry and polytheism as well as theological compromise (not
without some historical validity). But Roman Catholics too have followed the negative interpretation of this word in recent theology and
missiology. The first appendix to this volume examines these positions in more detail. But the license to proceed with such a study
demands a more explicit prefatory statement as a down-payment,
the coin of which consists, I believe, of the following complex of
impressions.

First, as most missiologists today have come to acknowledge, if the
gospel is to be embraced among new communities, it must be an
"inculturated"[1] gospel—a gospel incarnated within its new culture, or
"contextualized" within it, if one prefers that term. (For clarifications

1. Since this term figures so prominently in our entire discussion, I must clarify its
   definition at the outset, by turning to its origin. Pedro Arrupe, in response to
   multiple letters and wide consultation, wrote his letter "To the Whole Society"
   on the recently coined word "inculturation." There he defines it as, "...the
   incarnation of Christian life and of the Christian message in a particular cultural
   context, in such a way that this experience not only finds expression through

see Bevans, 1992, Schineller, 1990, Shorter, 1988, Peelman, 1988, Guillemette, 1995) The only alternative to an ethnocentric and imperialistic insistence that new Christians should also become European or North American in their cultural expressions and identity, is a process of inculturation, which cannot possibly proceed without syncretic practices and modes of thought. There are all too many embarrassing histories describing elaborate amalgams of Christian symbols and traditional "pagan" content that came about because of bad communication, which church officials seem to have chosen to ignore rather than to converse with them. One sign that such issues still are not being dealt with is that, after a quarter century of study and teaching on such issues, one finds that even long-term missionaries, graduate students and professional theologians display such highly uninformed viewpoints on intercultural experience. It has been the practice simply to hurl the accusation of "syncretism" at most attempts to create syntheses of religious experience. Such protestations come from both the "liberal" and "conservative" wings of the churches, and demonstrate little study of the literature on the issue.

Secondly, the problem is hardly just a missiological one. The history of doctrinal and liturgical development since the first century manifests how fine the distinction is between syncretism and theological synthesis of Christian and "pagan" elements. As we shall discuss later, these syntheses were most obviously meetings between the proclaimers of the gospel and their Roman and/or Hellenistic environment. But deeper study (of which we will be able to see only some examples) has shown an equally powerful influence from the cultures of the Middle East, the Horn of Africa, North Africa, and various areas of northern Europe, most especially what are now Ireland and the areas of continental Europe once known as "Germanic." All of these developments contain profound syncretic characteristics, some of them dealt with in refined and meticulous fashion, such as among the early apologists and church Fathers. Other positions are

---

elements proper to the culture in question (this alone would be no more than superficial adaptation), but becomes a principle that animates, directs, and unifies the culture, transforming and remaking it so as to bring about 'a new creation'." (Arrupe, 1978)

less explicitly worked out, such as in the case of symbolism and teaching of the faith among the Franks, Goths, Saxons and Scandinavians.

Thirdly, we must not fail to note that there have indeed been crude and dehumanizing forms of syncretism that Christian leaders failed to recognize and discern. These forms led to some of the worst horrors to emerge in the modern world. Just to point out some of these for the sake of dramatic effect here, one thinks of the Emperor Theodosius's Edict of Thessalonica in 381, establishing and enforcing Christianity as the state religion. In this ironic but predictable turn of events, Christianity passed from its status as a persecuted minority through acceptance as one of the "licit" religions under Constantine, to become the official religion of the Empire (MacMullen, 1997, Cc.1 and 2). This was not simply a political movement; it was a form of religious syncretism that mingled ancient Roman belief in divine patronage with the new belief in The God of Christianity. Soon following suit was the conversion of the Frankish chieftain Clovis in 492, initiating the development of a northern brand of caesaropapism that culminated in the ninth century rule of Charlemagne, who then forced religious conformity on the Saxons. By this time, too, the religious spirit inherent in feudal loyalty was developing, and was to culminate in the religious syncretism known as the Crusades. By this means, the Church was able to effect a certain peace among the warring tribes of the north and redirect their energies against the religio-political threat of Islam in the south.

The prism of syncretism is also a valuable instrument for examining the practices of the Inquisition as it culminated in the seventeenth century. Founded, at least as argued by its defenders, to serve as an authentic guide to Christian thought and practice, it devolved into an amalgam of ecclesiastical authority and secular power, symbolized, for example, by Boniface VIII's *Unam Sanctam* in 1298. Being aware of the danger of over-generalization, one might nevertheless suggest that from this amalgam there ensued the increasingly complex syncretism that led to the destructive quarrels of the Reformation and Counterreformation. This warfare quickly embraced Caesar in his various guises, and culminated in the wars of religion, or Thirty Years War ending in 1648. Even the "secularization" that followed the Treaty of Westphalia and embraced early elements of Enlightenment freedom from religious authority led to a gross form of syncretism that enthroned the Goddess Reason during the French Revolution.

Recent history demonstrates two demonic forms of syncretism in the examples of *apartheid* and Nazism. Apartheid as a religious syncretism began when Dutch Reformed Christians, fleeing persecution in Europe, discovered the beautiful expanse of land in southern Africa that came to be known as The Republic of South Africa. In order to protect themselves from further harassment, they gradually established a religiopolitical system based in an eisegesis of parts of the Old Testament and in an ideology of racial separation, implicitly of racial superiority. It was only in the late twentieth century that the churches of South Africa declared this kind of syncretism a heresy. As for Nazism, which claimed to be the full realization of revelation, we are already sufficiently cognizant of its demonic nature.

It might be argued that all the theological issues around natural/ supernatural, grace/freedom, church/state, integrism, secularism, and others can be traced to problems symbolized by the word syncretism. However, in order to avoid an encyclopedic study of this one issue, this book will confine itself to an examination of syncretic process as it figures in the outreach of the Church into the non-Christian world. From that starting point, we will study the dialogue between the already existing Church and the so-called "young churches" growing out of the spread of Christianity beyond Europe. The intention here is not to argue necessarily for a total whitewashing of the term "syncretism" or for its canonization, but simply for its de-demonization. Thuswise might one hope to reconfigure the discussion through a recognition that syncretic process is inevitable in cross-cultural encounter and a process proper to a period of uncertainty, as Ulrich Berner has noted (Cited in Rudolph, 1979, 205). Thus it is a process calling both for patience and for careful dialogue. This dialogue will demand a phenomenological approach that leads to mutual discernment in the growth of authentic Christianity or at least to a responsible dialogue between the Church and traditions outside Christianity. The problems of syncretism represent at least one dramatic instance of the need for theology to appreciate the growth of human consciousness. Bernard Lonergan and his followers have called this "the data of consciousness" and "generalized empirical method" (Crowe, 1984, Lonergan, 1972, index). I have suggested that the syncretic process, at least within a mission context, might accept what I have inelegantly called the "theological messiness" that characterizes theology on the margins (Starkloff, 1994).

Finally, one might hope, as a result of these discussions, that the Church universal will "lift up" the leaders of the young churches to a respected and deserved role within the hermeneutical processes of doctrinal development. The meeting of minds between missionaries and native leaders in the past mission history of the Church have generally taken the form of "power encounters" and contests, as indeed such encounters will no doubt always be to some degree. The "contest" should take place, however, not between competing and warring sides, but between ideas and experiences which all might understand as part of a syncretic process leading to a healthy synthesis of Christian thought and praxis. We might thus hope that further encounters avoid the marginalization and identity conflicts suffered by local cultures at the hands of "catholic" Christianity.[2]

A further important note on terminology should be mentioned. Regardless of the definitions and usages employed by the various authors whom I will cite in this book, my own meanings will be, as consistently as possible with such elusive terminology, the following. When I use the word "syncretism," I will intend the more "spontaneous" aspect of religious mingling, without necessarily any intention of a pejorative meaning. Rudolph characterizes this spontaneity as the "unconscious" type of syncretism (Rudolph, 1979, 207). The word "synthesis" will denote the more reflective and deliberative combinations such as have occurred under intellectual leadership throughout history. The phrase "syncretic process" will be used to describe any generic phenomenon of historical amalgamation, usually a combination of the other two terms, which emphasizes the dynamic nature of syncretism.

From the very outset of Christianity, its leaders counselled their followers to "test the spirits to see if they are of God." (1 Jn.4:1; 1 Thess.5:21) Many of Paul's struggles and those of the Johannine writer

---

2. This is one of the major themes of the excellent anthology, *Suchbewegungen*, (Siller, 1991) which I discuss in greater detail in Appendix I.

called for the practice of the discernment of spirits within many manifestations of culture and religion. In other words, the leaders of the Church, without ever recording the word, were wrestling with the problem of syncretism. Thus, the fundamental theme of the present book holds that this same process continues to characterize Christian theology today, and will do so until the "recapitulation of all things in Christ." Thus, the name later given to this phenomenon—syncretism—describes a process that will endure as long as history endures.

The purpose of theology in this process is to discern the truth to be found within history. The title of this book contains a reference to the phrase "In-Between," and, anticipating a later discussion of the concept, I introduce it here in order to describe the process in which we are involved. The idea of the "In-Between" fascinated the great polymath Eric Voegelin, as he struggled to interpret the quest of humankind (or at least of western civilization) to understand the meaning of history and to find order within it. While he did occasionally use the word "syncretism" to describe aspects of culture, he never disputed its usage, but chose another term—in most instances a rather innocuous preposition used in the classics—to symbolize the period of historical tension between the beginning and the end. He called this condition "the Metaxy." For example, Augustine's tension between the *Civitas Dei* and the *Civitas Terrena*, was a metaxy that would be paradigmatic for centuries to come, a state of the tension in history between the powers of heaven and earth. (Voegelin, 1974, 172)

Prior even to Augustine, wrote Voegelin, St. Paul proclaimed the Resurrection as the event in the divine-human metaxy that would constitute meaning in history (1974, 243). In the introduction to Volume Five of Voegelin's monumental *Order in History*, Ellis Sandoz described Voegelin's metaxy as the realm of "participatory existence," or humans sharing in the saving power of grace. (Voegelin, 1987, 1) Here Voegelin is described as seeking in a mystic fashion to restore appreciation of the place of historic tension within society. (1987, 12). Voegelin himself described the metaxy as "...the symbol that validly expresses the experience of existence in the Between of thing-reality, including the bodily location of consciousness, and of Beyond-reality..." (Voegelin, 1987, 30) It is the experience of a historically situated hunger for eternity.

Voegelin argued that humans, through their imaginative respon-
siveness, are creative partners in the movement of reality toward truth.
Humankind's perpetual paradoxical relationship to syncretism (which
Voegelin frequently used to describe different efforts towards unity
within diversity), is summed up thusly: "The conflict between the
plurality of ecumenic ages and the universality of mankind originates in the In-Between of existence" (Voegelin, 1987,304). In other
words, it is the fate of humankind to search for its longed-for unity
amid the constant tensions of diversity and therefore conflict, from
the earliest philosophers to the present day. We shall visit the concept
of metaxy more at length later, but I introduce it here in order to
furnish us with a dynamic symbol for the study of syncretism in
which we are engaged. If we are to interpret syncretism creatively, we
must put aside any static understanding of it and grasp its constantly
tensive character. To that end we shall first examine the history of
syncretism as it developed with the spread of Christianity from its
middle-eastern origin into the continent of Europe.

I

THE EUROPEAN EPOCH:
THE METAXY BETWEEN 100 AND 1300

Among the hundreds of articles written by Karl Rahner, few have received as much "mileage" as a relatively brief one, originally a public lecture: "Towards a Fundamental Theological Interpretation of Vatican II." (K. Rahner, 1979) This address has captured many imaginations with its simple division of Christian history into three cultural "epochs"—the brief Jewish epoch, the European epoch that has endured for two millennia, and the "world church" epoch that began in a halting way with the Second Vatican Council. For the purpose of the present book, I offer here an overview of the synthetic, or indeed syncretic, process during the formative period running from the earliest apologists through the thirteenth century and the scholastic synthesis that reached its apogee with Thomas Aquinas.

Not to deny the continuity of further syncretic process beyond this time, of course, it is arguably valid to state that the major developments of the European synthesis had been assembled with the end of the high scholastic period. I would be far from denying the enormous impact of the Reformation and the Enlightenment on this process, but neither of these, for all their influence, transcended the European culture of their origins. My point here is to highlight the major syncretistic factors that could eventually lead Hilaire Belloc to announce that "Europe is the faith, and the faith is Europe."

We are still at this point within the "phenomenological" stage of our discussion; that is, we seek to refrain from the judgments proper to systematic and pastoral theology and to construct an accurate description of the development of syncretic processes. This does not however, forbid the "naming" of phenomena, and my first assignment of a name to describe this historical process is that of Voegelin's

"Metaxy"—the "In-Between"—which I will now describe in greater detail. This word appears in the writings of Plato and Aristotle, though perhaps without the heavy connotations given it by Voegelin. However, Aristotle , in his *Metaphysics*, 987b, 14-18, discusses how Plato used the Greek preposition to describe the intermediate position occupied by the forms, between sensible experience and eternal reality. This description seems to be what Voegelin chose in seeking for a description of the historical period of creative tension in humankind's ceaseless quest for the meaning of history—even before the passage into the conscious phase that we call history today. In one sense, the entire human story is a metaxy, but we can use Voegelin's terminology to describe the period in which Christians have struggled to discover, or to uncover, the dynamic of the eternal gospel as it transforms cultures.

Among other great philosophers of history, R.G. Collingwood recognized the power of Christianity for historiography in its three qualities—universal consciousness, providential guidance, and an intelligible pattern of events (Collingwood, 1946, 49-50). The Christian sense of a backward and a forward sense in history, at least as early as Bede, characterizes the Christian historian's ability to isolate meaningful epochs and periods, all focused on the Christ-event. These three qualities apply dramatically to the metaxic period that I am about to describe.

But what exactly is the creative power of Voegelin's version of the Metaxy for capturing the historical imagination? Throughout his massive *Order in History*, the various cultural strivings to discern order within developing reality, from the ancient Egyptians through the period of the Old Testament and that of Greek tragedy and philosophy, are all metaxic. Each period is fraught with the tension of creative imagination and intense longing for meaning. In Christian history, which is our interest here of course, Voegelin cites the Resurrection as the one event in the Metaxy that gives meaning to history itself (Voegelin, 1974, 243). The Metaxy is the "In-Between" of participatory existence (that is, of the Platonic participation in saving power) where the divine and the human meet. Voegelin, writes Ellis Sandoz in the introduction to the fifth volume of *Order and History*, found mystical prayer, as he understood it from *The Cloud of Un-*

knowing, to have the potential "to restore the problem of the Metaxy for society and history" (In Voegelin, 1987, 1). To paraphrase Voegelin further, the Metaxy is the symbol that expresses humankind's condition as being in the body but conscious of the Beyond (Voegelin, 1987, 30). In this state, human beings are participators in the movement of reality toward truth.

What does this mean as we pursue the study of syncretism? Voegelin tells us, toward the end of his fourth volume, that "the conflict between the plurality of ecumenic ages and the universality of mankind originates in the In-Between of existence" (304). In other words, the attempts of humans to achieve a unity of opposites, even of contradictions, in religious experience are part of the quest for final unification. Syncretism, we may say, is part of the eschatological quest, and it is part of Voegelin's contribution that he denied (as did Kierkegaard against Hegel) that humankind would ever perfectly "mediate" or solve this tension by means of speculation (50).

One of Voegelin's commentators has pointed out how that philosopher considered it necessary for the gospel to merge with Greek philosophy in order to become the cultural force that it was meant to be (Douglas, 1978, 140). For this critic, Voegelin had missed the whole meaning of gospel as salvation, but in his defense of its cultural value he did succeed in divorcing Christianity from Gnosticism—a type of syncretism that denied the metaxic principle by claiming to "solve" and put a premature end to the tension of existence (146).

Another commentator sees the metaxy as the context in which consciousness becomes luminous to itself by extending itself to participation with other units of consciousness (Corrington, 1978, 167). But again, in his opposition to Gnosticism, Voegelin saw all temporal existence as a tension in the quest for final unity. Thus, in his fourth volume, Voegelin could write, "The mankind whose humanity unfolds in the flux of presence is universal mankind, the universality of mankind is constituted by the divine presence in the Metaxy" (Corrington, 176; Voegelin, 1974, 304). This tension is an all-embracing historical, philosophical, theological, psychic, and spiritual condition that humans must negotiate throughout humankind's time in this world. The struggles connected with religious syncretism are foremost in the Christian experience (*at least* the Christian experience) of this tension.

THE CHURCH FATHERS

While the earliest apologists and theologians, Justin, Irenaeus and Clement of Alexandria, condemned in one voice the polytheism and idolatry of hellenistic culture, as well as its mystery religions, they also brooded over the mystery of salvation for the pagans. They pondered the kind of consciousness that would not only allow divine grace to reach them but could also bring that consciousness to bear on the Church's theological life (Dupuis, 1997, 53-83). I refer to their belief in the Cosmic Christ, the Word in the world from the beginning, the eternal divine *Logos* which has been manifesting itself in the world since the moment of creation. This was the position of Justin, who contemplated the *Logos* at work among Jews and Greeks prior to the Incarnation. Those who lived by the *Logos* would find salvation, as especially was true for Plato and Socrates. It was not merely the word of human reason that saved them, but the Christ Word himself from whom the saving word came.

During or shortly after the time of Justin, Irenaeus of Lyons typified the thinking we have described above as metaxic. As Jacques Dupuis interprets him, "...the historical work of Jesus Christ as Redeemer forms the mid-point of a line which leads from the Old Testament to the return of Christ" (Dupuis, 1997,60). Humans can reach the knowledge of God through the cosmos, not by their own power, but because creation is a divine manifestation. As Irenaeus himself wrote, "For by means of the creation itself, the world reveals God the Creator, and by means of the world (does he declare) the Lord, the maker of the world; and through that which is moulded, the artisan who moulded it; and by the Son the Father who begat the Son."(62; Ireneaus, *Against the Heresies*, IV, 6, 5-6) The Son who becomes the historical Christ is the ultimate visibility of the *Logos*.

Clement of Alexandria advanced the thought of Justin and Irenaeus by describing the *Logos* as extending his influence beyond the boundaries of the Judeo-Christian tradition to the "prophets" of the pagan world. Somehow the great philosophers in their search for truth found the blessing of divine assistance. As Dupuis writes, "Philosophy comes from God; it constitutes for the Greek world a divine economy, parallel if not in all things equal, to the Jewish economy of the Law, both now designed to lead people to Christ..." (Dupuis, 1997, 67). Philosophy is a covenant made by God with people as a "stepping stone" to Christ. Clement envisioned this mediation in the great philosophers of India as well, all of them led by the Word who finally is Christ.

This is just a brief summary of the famous apologetic for the *Logos*, as the Sower in Justin, as the Revealer in Irenaeus, as the Covenant in Clement. In each case thus far we are describing the divine activity preparing humans for the coming of Christ. Was this a form of syncretistic thought, or was it based entirely on "divine revelation"? Dupuis refuses to answer with a facile either/or, and argues that the Johannine prologue itself is an integration of philosophy with the Word of God acting in history (72). Thus too did the great apologists carry forward that integration, that synthesis, which we are calling the syncretic process. But, as Dupuis takes care to caution us, those fathers of the Church held fast to a fundamental principle underlying any hermeneutic of syncretism: the Logos is finally Christ, and in this sense the *Logos* integrates all the experience of the pagan philosophers. It seems evident that, at this early point in the Christian epoch of the Metaxy, its thinkers were accepting the syncretistic aspiration as a product of the human quest for grace, and not as the result of sin.

Does the syncretic process—the mixing of cultural and gentile spiritual elements with the Christian tradition—thus belong within the Christian theology of history? I maintain that it does, not only since the apologists, but since the period of the evangelists themselves, at least since the appearance the Johannine gospel. What the Johannine and some Pauline writings, as well as the earliest fathers were careful to distinguish, however, was the authentic synthesis of human knowledge and experience with the Word made flesh in Christ, from the heterodox syncretism of the Gnostics. As Jean Daniélou has written, the early apologists were seeking to show how Christianity was the authentic heir of Graeco-Roman civilization (Daniélou and Marrou, 1964, 92). Interpreting the work of Clement, he notes, "If Christianity spreads in the Greek world, it must doff its Semitic form and

put on a Hellenist form, it must speak the language of Plato and
Homer and take the attitudes of Hermes and Ulysses" (132). Early
Christian art, such as depicted on burial sarcophagi, used Greek models of death and resurrection, such as the return of Ulysses (Opposite
65 and 128). However, Clement sought to embrace this word only at
the level of symbols, images and customs; in his work was "no trace
of syncretism" (132). That is, there was no reduction of the Christian
message to Greek mythology. A similar process of synthesis (reflectively syncretic) is found in the work of Tertullian, who introduced
Roman legal thought and terminology into theology, as well as the
language of Roman military patriotism (Evans, 1972, 19).

Hugo Rahner's great work, *Greek Myths and Christian Mystery*, provides a wealth of detail to describe this process of "transposition" of
Christian meaning into pagan forms. All the Hellenistic symbols
became candidates for baptism, starting with the idea of "mystery"
itself (H. Rahner, 1963, xviii) and moving to the numerology of the
Pythagoreans and to Greek and Roman solar and lunar mythology.
Greek imagery that focused on organic metaphors, such as the wil-
low tree as symbol of virginity or the herbs given by Hermes to
Odysseus as protection against the charms of Circe, became images
to be transformed by the *Logos* (223). The ship of Odysseus, who
ordered himself tied to its mast, lest he yield to the song of the Sirens,
becomes a symbol of the Church guiding us to our heavenly home
(Ch. VII).

The Church embraced an even wider assortment of pagan elements,
such as Stoicism, various forms of Platonism, and the mystery religions, while maintaining the Jewish religion of righteousness. It transformed Syrian asceticism and dualism, Roman ideas of sin and salvation, as well as church administration, and eventually absorbed the
rationalism of Aristotle. As J.H. Randall sees it, far from being a
corruption of the gospel, all of these developments constituted an
enrichment, all accomplished by what he ironically calls one generation after another of "modernists" (Randall, 1970, 138).

Another scholar, Ramsay MacMullen, has devoted a recent book
to illustrating the degree to which paganism survived within Christianity itself, especially during the "dark ages" period (MacMullen,
1997, 1-2 and *passim*). While Hugo Rahner is much more cautious

about the syncretic process, he would agree with Randall and MacMullen to this extent:

> The Church was not fashioned in a vacuum; it is the continuation of God's becoming man; it must therefore turn to man with the revelation that Christ entrusted to it—and all that means that, at the time, it had to turn to the men of the Graeco-Roman world with their distinctive speech and culture" (H. Rahner, 1963, 13).

In the growth of its worship, Christianity turned constantly to pagan symbolism, as one of the great historians of liturgy writes. (Jungmann, 1959). From the era of Constantine, especially, it drew numerous developments, such as the basilica form of architecture, Graeco-Roman prayer styles, a synthesis of Greek ostentation and Roman conciseness, pagan art depicting all of life's realities, and the orientation of prayer to the East. The use of milk and honey in the baptism ceremony was a hellenistic inclusion, as was the floral wreathe at weddings, the *refrigerium* or meal for and with the dead, and, of course, the eventual connection of the Lord's birthday with the Roman feast of the Unconquered Sun. The Greek mystery cults themselves, as manifestations of the desire for salvation, had to be recognized as a quest for an eternal goal similar to that of Christianity. Jungmann reasons, "Christian culture and pagan culture cannot be considered so completely antagonistic to one another as to make any compromises impossible, compromises in the field of literature, compromises in the field of the arts" (133). The remnants were to be refashioned, not destroyed, as the whole pagan world was called to enter the Kingdom of God.

Discerning an Authentic Process

Protestants and Catholics will differ over how to interpret the distinction between legitimate syncretic process and an indiscriminate "mishmash" in all of this history, and the issue will occupy our attention in a later chapter. However, it must be asked at this point in the early phase of Karl Rahner's "second epoch," how Christian leadership sought to discern an appropriate praxis. For example, what about Christianity's distinctiveness over-against the various forms of gnosticism, which were already elaborate syncretisms before Christianity arrived? As Daniélou describes it, Christianity adopted hellenistic culture just as eastern Gnosticism did, but each maintained its appropriate truths (Daniélou, 1964,134). Manicheeism, for example, retained Persian dualism while it embraced Greek symbolism. Christianity clung to its biblical roots with even greater tenacity as a reaction to this, and early Christian leaders, according to Jungmann, struggled against the influence of Gnosticism in worship (Jungmann, 1959, Ch. 10).

Clearly, Gnosticism was perhaps the most dramatic foil of Christianity in its efforts to practice authentic syncretic reflection, or synthesis. But what *was* Gnosticism and how can we learn from it in defining the difference between a genuine Christian syncretic process and uncritical syncretism? Jungmann writes, "Its origins must be sought in the religious syncretism which, from the time of Alexander's conquests and still more the Roman subjugation, had mingled and fused the many oriental cults (110). Kurt Rudolph calls Gnosis "...a product of hellenistic syncretism, that is the mingling of Greek and oriental traditions and ideas subsequent to the conquests of Alexander the Great" (Rudolph, 1983, 54). Gnosis sought to embrace all forms of wisdom, thus uniting in itself many aspects of the Gnostic view of the world, with both its positive and negative qualities. Following the history-of-religions school of thought, Rudolph sees Gnosticism as a pre-Christian movement that gradually enriched itself with Christian concepts, rather than as a Christian heresy. For Rudolph, Gnosticism should be analyzed without any attempt to evaluate it, since, as a very vital syncretism it simply shares the identity of all other religions, which in some way too are syncretistic (286).

However, Rudolph turns to a description of the Christian "symbiosis" with Gnosticism: "The process which is plain from the New Testament itself is twofold, the Christianizing of Gnosis and the gnosticizing of Christianity" (300). From the point that begins to manifest the tensions in Pauline and Johannine writings, the struggle for Christian uniqueness is dramatically evident. Christianity *is* a "religion of salvation" as is Gnosticism, but it is also very different. Rudolph mentions the teachings of Ignatius of Antioch in the early second century as an effort to combat Gnosticism through his appeals to church unity around the bishops (303). In general, Rudolph is critical of these "heresiological" fathers of the Church, especially Justin, Ireneaus and Clement, for their excessive polemics against Gnosticism, which diminish the value of their very valid criticisms of it.

Elaine Pagels's widely recognized book, *The Gnostic Gospels*, focuses more specifically on the polemics between orthodox Christians and the Gnostics. Like Rudolph, Pagels has taken a historical approach and striven to study Gnosticism objectively in order to explore the evidence phenomenologically. While she emphasizes that there were many gnostic traditions, she neither agrees nor disagrees with Rudolph that these groups were pre-Christian, simply citing historians who hold the independent and pre-Christian origins of the movement. While not siding with the Gnostics, Pagels regrets the intemperate treatment accorded them by the early Fathers, who thus forced them to the margins and out of the communion to which they might have made some contribution (Pagels, 1979, 151).

Pagels's observations deserve consideration in this investigation, since she herself ultimately maintains her allegiance to historical Christianity, but points out the need for careful examination of the evidence and for discernment. No doubt, as in so many strife-ridden periods of Christian history, such objectivity was hard to muster during those early centuries. In any case, the early period is a striking instance of the tensions of Voegelin's metaxic quest for order and meaning in history.

When we turn to the intentional and reflective labors of Christian writers to deal with the conflicts described above, we begin to detect patterns of discernment. These patterns focus on the confession of Jesus Christ as the Word Incarnate and on the unity of the Christian confession. But even in these cases, the processes are syncretic, drawing upon traditions in many ways at odds among themselves. As the late nineteenth century scholar Edwin Hatch argued, Christianity first learned to use its wings during an age of moral reform in its Mediterranean environment among Stoics, Cynics and Neo-Platonists. One of its greatest apologists, Origen, built upon Greek cosmogony as "a reasoned basis for Hebrew monotheism" (Hatch, 1907, 207), just as the early liturgical leaders drew upon the myster-

ies of Greek culture. What for Hatch is the authenticating criterion
in all these developments is the "catholic," or universal faith professed in a doctrine coordinated with the life of the world around it
(345).

Andrew Walls cites the turn of first generation Christians to the
pagan Greek title of "Lord" to describe Jesus, in spite of the fear
many of them had of the "syncretistic possibilities" in this. (Walls,
1997, 148) But many similar turns moved the Church toward three
stages in the conversion of Hellenistic thought. There was first a missionary stage that adopted certain gnostic conceptions such as *pleroma*
to describe Christ, for example. There was then a convert stage, typified by Justin, who was and had to be a Greek philosopher and not a
Hebrew, one who could employ the concept of *Logos* not only as
Word but as Reason. In a third, or refiguration, stage, Origen saw his
work as an act of "spoiling the Egyptians" by the use of materials
taken from the heathen world, fashioning them into objects used to
worship the one God (149).

Christian thought further appropriated two other areas of intellectual activity—law and historical writing. The first legal language, as
has been noted in the case of Tertullian and Cyprian, was that of
Roman law, until Christianity moved north and adopted forms of
law peculiar to Anglo-Saxon or Germanic models. In the realm of
historiography, Walls cites Bede's work in the ninth century, which
inserted the historical sequence into the usage of the A.D. dating
system. On the continent, Isidore of Seville composed a historical
methodology for his own Gothic people in which he successfully
urged Gothic kings to submit themselves to the one King, Christ
(152).

If the centrality of Christ as Word Incarnate was one major element to distinguish Christianity from the uncorseted syncretism of
the Gnostics, the belief in the unity of the Church was another. In
his famous early nineteenth century masterwork, *The Unity of the
Church*, the tragically short-lived Tübingen Catholic theologian and
ecumenist, Johann Adam Möhler, described in great detail how the
early Fathers, especially Cyprian, struggled for unity, and in the process he sets forth criteria for judging authentic syncretic processes
from crude syncretism. Möhler wrote, "The early Christians were

not satisfied in any way with a mere statement that the Christian religious *concepts* were better than pagan ones. They did not want Christianity to be received after a mere comparison of concepts, or that it be chosen for this reason" (Möhler, 1996, 91). Rather, the pagan must take on a Christian way of life and this must be a shared inner life, a life of holy power. "And all doctrinal concepts and dogmas have value only insofar as they express the inner life that is present with them" (111). Möhler cites especially the work of Justin and Clement of Alexandria for their quest after such a wholistic unity within a "Christian philosophy" (74-75).

Möhler also recognized that from the time of the apostles there was a willingness to accept diverse forms within this unity of the Spirit. Pagan symbols were no more to be shunned than were Jewish ones:

> The Christian Church could thus accept pagan symbols (indeed, prayer formulae such as the *Kyrie*) if they were exceptional and a Christian idea could be found with them. To attack the Church because of this is the result of both Gnostic and Pharisaic narrowness... the principle of unity stood above forms, and in all its movements it resulted in nothing other than expressing *one* spirit in many forms" (203).

While Möhler of course represented the Roman Catholic side of the ecumenical dialogue, his emphatic endorsement of collegial government and collaboration was a prophetic clarion whose message died with him and was revived only by some theologians preparing for Vatican Council II. The point in noting this here is that the various syncretic processes involved in Möhler's historical description maintain their Christian authenticity through a dialogue carried on in unity.

Within a series of "*Addenda*" to his text, Möhler especially notes the value of Origen's frequent utilization of the method of allegorical exegesis drawn from pagan Greek writings, especially of Hesiod and Homer (289). While he notes that much of Origen's writing in the third century is of little use in our own times, Origen's accomplishment in his own time was to build a bridge to a deeper meaning for the text of Holy Scripture (295). In this same spirit, he also adds an

appendix "On the Salvation of the Pagans," which echoes the thought
of Justin and Irenaeus (355). The philosophy which served the *Logos*
as a means of the salvation of the ancients is not of evil origin, "since
it makes human beings virtuous. It is of divine origin since God can
only do good deeds." In such wise Clement of Alexandria could as-
cribe to philosophy a justifying power, but only as directing us to the
Lord himself (357). On the other hand, Greek and eastern philosophies, when they fell into Gnosticism, simply seized upon Christianity as a vehicle for their speculations, rather than as the communion
of the Spirit. They sought simply to either satisfy curiosity or to free
some hidden kernel of rational truth from the biblical husks. (394)
In other words, Möhler would see an inauthentic syncretism as the
source of heresy because it loses touch with the Incarnation, the Spirit
and the unity of the Body.

Among the early theologians cited often by Möhler, four stand out
as representatives of the authentic syncretic process: I mean the
Cappadocians Gregory of Nyssa, Basil of Caesarea, Gregory
Nazianzen, and (at least as Jaroslav Pelikan believes) Macrina, the
sister of the first two. According to Pelikan's account, these theologians are synthesists striving to integrate the gospel with their own
hellenistic culture, a practice that they saw symbolized and justified
by the fact that the New Testament was written in *koiné* Greek. They
were the first exponents of a certain "natural theology" that grows
out of a dialogue between Revelation and the Greek quest for reasoned discourse (Pelikan, 1993, 21). But far from the rationalism
that natural theology is sometimes believed to be, theirs was a vision
of Christian Platonism that was separated from early Platonism by
an immense difference—the difference represented by faith in a source
outside of pure reason. The chief adversary of the Cappadocians was
the "recrudescent paganism" of the Emperor Julian (perhaps unfairly
called "the apostate"), who, like many of our contemporary partners
among aboriginal peoples, wanted nothing to do with "syncretism,"
seeking rather to restore a primitive (but nonetheless syncretistic)
form of Graeco-Roman religion. This was Julian's form of orthodoxy
against which these theologians waged their own defense of Christian orthodoxy—the wedding of biblical faith and hellenistic reason.

For the Cappadocians, drawing upon their great predecessor, Origen, natural theology became "not only an apologetic but a presupposition for systematic, dogmatic theology" (38). Out of this viewpoint emerged the "chief dogma" of the Church, the Nicene Creed. But the very language of the Creed manifests the most un-gnostic of beliefs: the transcendence of God places theology within a quest to respond to the One who is beyond all Greek ideas of divinity. A key element of Greek linguistic culture shows itself here in a linguistic detail; the "alpha privitive" in patristic lexicons expresses more what God is *not* than *what* God is (40). However, needing some language basis, they spoke of the divine as "light from light," and as *Logos (44)*. Their Christian Platonism found further expression in a certain "Christian Socratism" that worked from a "turn to the subject" expressed in Socrates's Delphic Oracle testimony, "Know thyself" (121). From one's own self-knowledge, joined to the experience of faith, the Cappadocians could build a certain "proof" of God's existence that still confesses our ignorance of God's true nature—our *apophasis* about God (70).

In their opposition to Julian's polytheistic syncretism, these theologians strove to keep "nature" in its own place; idolatry, such as in Julian's sun-worship, for example, was the cardinal disorder of identifying God with the forces of the universe. However, these four thinkers manifest the quality, in the language I am proposing in this book, of a discerning and reasoned discourse, a syncretic process. For example, they created a Christian cosmology out of the stuff of scriptural testimony and Greek philosophy, seeing the universe as a divinely grounded *order* over against *chaos*, an order governed by God as both Creator and Judge. God is the ruler of the space and time that we experience through our senses; the *Logos* respects the testimony of sense but transcends it (108-109). Out of Socratic self-knowledge grows an anthropology that views the human as micro-cosmos. Humans possess the ability to be microcosms because they are in the image of God; human nature is understood as a synthesis of Platonic, Stoic and Aristotelian world views joined to the Christian (121-125). Humans are gifted with reason, free will and immortality as the essential content of the image of God, but for these theologians this is arrived at only through faith in the resurrection (134). In the mystical thought of Macrina, "The doctrine of the natural immortality of the soul ... strikingly illustrated the complex relation between natural theology and revealed theology, or between Christianity and classical culture" (132).

The Christian syncretic process also progressed far along the path toward a biblical morality aided by Greek categories. But the Christian method and criteria are consistent: the testimony of scripture governs the procedure. Thus, for example, preceding the arguments of Las Casas by some twelve centuries, Basil and Gregory rejected Aristotle's teaching that any human could be a slave by nature, and Gregory rejected the belief that there was a double standard for sexual morality governing men and women (147-148). Likewise, Macrina argued, based on faith, that nature itself grasps the synthesis between classical and Christian virtues (136-137). The sovereignty of revelation shows itself in this synthesis in the precedence given to purpose over chaos—to *telos* over *tyché*, in the light of which the Cappadocians could emphasize freedom and purpose over fate or determinism. Our contemporary post-Christian view imposes a rather severe "hermeneutic of suspicion" in this matter, but these early theologians, emerging from so many years of struggle and persecution, saw the triumph of Constantine and the eventual repression of heresy to be a political symbol of the Graeco-Christian synthesis. However, these same theologians also considered their efforts at synthesis of faith and reason to be the antithesis to fideism as well.

The role of natural theology as a presupposition to Christian theology rendered "orthodoxy" a "royal road" between the two opposed cultures of Hellenism and Judaism. But what *was* orthodoxy for these fourth century thinkers? Certainly, they would agree with their predecessors that the unity of the Church is a key to discernment here, but Basil emphasized the role of collaboration between the human spirit and the divine Spirit in correlating "what was gathered from Holy Scripture" and "received from the unwritten tradition of the fathers." Natural theology is of some value, but it must finally profess *apophasis* in relation to pure reason, and accept the actions of the Church and the creeds. This they saw to be the process of Christian theology (195).

Faith, as should be evident by now, was for the Cappadocians the fulfillment of reason. Macrina saw the pedagogical power of the *Logos* to be the expression of *Sophia*, which she equated with the second person of the Trinity, although the understanding of scripture must again be given by divine wisdom rather than by any philosophical training. Thus, the Nicene Creed itself had to recognize a certain *apophasis* as it distinguished how divine fatherhood and sonship differ from human. It turned to the language of transcendence in order to free its trinitarian confession from any hint of polytheism.

The same sense of transcendence governs the fourth century theology of the cosmos: creation is contingent, governed by the divine "economy," with all things held together in Christ, according to the mystical vision of Macrina (155). The Greek word "economy" finds is full meaning in the Incarnation, creating a new language about the events of salvation (265). Through the Incarnation, human nature finds its metamorphosis in the process of *theosis* that frees it from the disfigurement of sin, a category that serves as a further criterion for distinguishing the supremacy of faith in its correlation with reason. Faith in turn leads to worship (*lex orandi lex credendi*), and is intimately united with ethics, with the practice of the love of God and love of neighbor which will finally accompany all into the life of the world to come, where there will finally be a full metamorphosis of knowledge. As Pelikan summarizes all of this historical process, the Cappadocians' adherence to perfection was a "universalism" that sought to comprehend Christianity and classical culture within a single system (312). As Daniélou put it, this was the beginning of a flowering of Christian culture, by means of unexpected transpositions and applications. "Christianity was the leading principle of the *Zeitgeist*, of the cultural atmosphere of the century (Daniélou and Marrou, 1964, 302).

Passage

Let us summarize here the synthetic movement as it passed through the formative stage of the patristic period. It is a process beginning within the Bible itself, which developed the doctrinal content to which all Christians are heirs, regardless of differences of interpretation. Later in this book, we shall examine a theory of doctrine and how it applies to syncretic process, but at this point it will be of help to pause long enough to restate basic doctrinal points that apply to problems arising in the context of syncretism.

"Syncretic processes and synthetic processes are likely the same," Robert Schreiter has suggested (Schreiter, 1997, 71). Certainly, at least, the relationship between the two is analogous. In any case, something must be said here about the agents of this process in metaxic history. The great theologians in the history of the Church, from its very beginnings, have been cultured and educated thinkers with a keen eye to the ways in which elements from their "high culture" (basically philosophy but also art and poetry) might be synthesized to engage in a hermeneutic of the Christian tradition. Our work on syncretism as understood by those who must deal with it today carries us into other cultures and indeed into the ranks of other types of cultural leaders. These are leaders who build and develop their cultures via methods differing sharply from those of the scholars who joined Christianity with hellenistic culture. I call these leaders *bricoleurs*, following the lead of writers in the Siller symposium discussed in Appendix I (Cf. Greverus, in Siller, 1991, 18-30). These writers themselves draw the term from Claude Levi-Strauss, who coined the word to apply to local religious leaders who make creative use of symbols by "puttering" with them in such a way as to provide others with living experiences (Levi-Strauss, 1966, Ch. 1, at 16-21). While it will be to such local leaders that we turn in missiological discourse, the developments to be examined in medieval northern Europe will bear a striking resemblance to the activity called *bricolage*. As in any examination of mission the question arises: What are the fundamental elements of early Christianity that must interact with other cultures without any sacrifice of true Christian identity?

First, as we have seen from the struggles of the Church with gnosticism, those early leaders preserved the value of "knowing" within their faith, albeit not from independent speculation but from reflection on a common witness. Thus, an inheritance from the early apologists is our treasure of a saving message that somehow "recapitulates" all that is good in the pagan philosophies. But all of these theologians, in their speculations and witnessing, are concerned with the value of ecclesial *unity*.

But unity alone is hardly sufficient, since there can indeed be a unity that destroys as well as saves. Christian unity among the early patristic theologians, already heir to the credal formulations, has to be grounded in the confession of the Word made flesh, in the Incarnation as it would be finally defined at Chalcedon and refined in later councils prior to the eighth century. Against Gnosticism, these leaders had to emphasize the bodily as well as the eternal-transcendent nature of Jesus, and thus the wholistic character of his redemptive work in the world. It was the work of those early councils to summarize this doctrinal unity.

The work of the Cappadocians is the growth of doctrine developed out of their conflicts, especially as represented by Julian's efforts to revitalize pagan culture against the Christian faith, and to absorb Christianity into Roman culture as one more of its elements. As Pelikan has indicated, Julian was indeed an early syncretist who, in the words of Siller, sought to reverse "subject" and "predicate": that is, he made culture the subject-agent of integration, with Christianity as its predicate. The labors of Basil, the two Gregories, and Macrina sought to integrate the faith with reason in such a way that reason was the servant of the Word, and to create a cosmology that achieved in a Christian and revolutionary way what Julian sought to achieve in a reactionary manner. Gregory of Nyssa especially sought to give the Church a "lexicon of transcendence" that integrated the faith of the Nicene Creed with reason and its best hellenistic expressions. His became a cosmology as well as an ethic that was based on the biblical doctrine of creation. In sum, what these theologians passed on to us out of their synthetic processes is the faith of the great creeds, summations of a faith that would be passed on to other cultures.

Along with creed, the community developed *cult*, or worship. We have seen through the work of Jungmann how the Church gradually took on elements of the pagan world that would contribute rich esthetic life to sacramental experience and faith, especially in Baptism and the Eucharist. Here as well, the Church had to do battle with gnostic teaching and practices to overcome both a disembodied version of worship as well as a distortion of ritual practices, such as in the controversy over relics, which were often obtained by gross and disedifying measures. Basically, the Christian principle that comes down to us, again with varieties of Christian interpretations of course, is that the elements of the good earth must all be part of the constitution of authentic worship.

In summary of the inheritance of early Christianity, then, the missionary Church received a heritage of what has often been called "creed, code and cult"—a tradition of faith, moral integrity and worship. In general, these are the elements that would have to be dealt with by means of theological and pastoral method as the Church sought to enunciate its gospel traditions out of its own hellenistic heritage, to tribal cultures that it would meet in its expansion into the barbarian frontiers of northern Europe. Out of this expansion, in its authentic communication of the gospel as well as its sometimes tragic distortions of the gospel, would arise many ongoing problems of syncretism.

To further forestall any triumphalism or any naive optimism about the syncretic process,[1] it will be helpful to bear in mind the many unfortunate accretions that would characterize the later European "Christendom," which would itself require many correctives. These correctives would be reforms such as those demanded by Las Casas and his later successors in liberation theology, by the Reformation, and eventually by the decisions of the Second Vatican Council and the World Council of Churches. We shall enter into that movement in the following chapter, but there is yet one more historical survey to record—that of the dynamics that synthesized or syncretized the Graeco-Roman/Germanic fusion that occurred between the fifth and the thirteenth centuries. Such a survey will deepen our understanding of the syncretic process that shows the Metaxy in both its tensions and its creativity. This investigation will uncover deeper analogues between our contemporary problems in cross-cultural mis-

---

1. For the sake of clarity, we are understanding the highly subtle difference between syncretism and synthesis as that between spontaneity and reflection. In other words, the syncretistic factor of any mingling of elements is the non-reflective side, while the synthetic factor is the product of more considered reflection, such as we saw in the case of the Cappadocians. Again, as Schreiter has remarked, an easy distinction is hard to come by!

sion and those that arose with the passage of the Church into the northern European tribal cultures.

CONTACT WITH THE BARBARIAN TRIBES

R.G. Collingwood (1956, 49-50) suggests four characteristics of Christian historiography, which I cite in support of the belief that ongoing syncretic process is a providential one, however flawed by human imperfection. Christian history-writing is thus described as: 1) universal in orientation, 2) guided by providence, 3) discerning of an intelligible pattern in events, and 4) future-oriented toward further epochs and events. Collingwood's basic schema had been first inaugurated by two early historiographers of northern Europe, Bede the Venerable and Isidore of Seville. That is, all history is directed toward the Christ-event, and henceforth derived from it. The Christian historian must beware of allowing his or her reading of data to be prejudiced by this fundamental belief, because it is indeed a belief and not an empirical certitude. But, appreciating the privilege of having such a point of interpretation, we maintain it in this historical analysis.

Accordingly, as we move into the northern sphere, we are conscious of the constant thrust of Christian faith and practice toward the universal inclusion of all nations. Thus, we seek to discern how Providence may be guiding the syncretic events described by historians, through an understanding of the intelligible patterns in them, by discerning the elements of light and darkness in a spirit of hope that, as we note in the thought of Moltmann, can alone save us from the destructive and uncritical aspects of the syncretic process. We have just examined how the great theologians of the patristic period endeavored to establish criteria for discernment—unity in diversity, divine transcendence, the Incarnation and the Trinity, the inclusion of all creation, and the unity of faith and reason as embodied in the early symbols. Related to these, there are the further elements of freedom and purpose versus determinism and fate, the unity of the Church under authority (obviously an issue still needing so much attention within the Christian family today), the reality of sin and the hope of redemption, and the "worship practiced by rational creatures" (Romans 12:1) through both prayer and the moral life.

Another English historian, Christopher Dawson, described "the making of Europe" as a process occurring in the period (much-maligned, as he believed) of the "dark ages." Given Dawson's heavily Catholic bias and his perhaps overly optimistic assessment of European unity, one may arguably agree with him on the ultimate unity of medieval culture and medieval religion (Dawson, 1936, xvii). To acquire a sense of that process we are seeking to understand, it may help simply to examine the illustrations in Dawson's book, which begins with a frontispiece called "the New People" found in the Roman catacombs, showing a fusion of the "New Man" theme that combined Christian faith with hellenistic art. Opposite page 64 there is a photo of the statue of "Christus Rhetor," embodying the Christian ideal with Greek secular thought in the area of eloquence. A frieze from Asia Minor, depicting "the king and the god" (105), is not a Christian image but a symbol of Persian culture's resistance to the hegemony of the west. The famous mosaic of San Vitale in Ravenna depicts the Byzantine Christ (*Pantocrator*) (opp. 120)—"a triumphal expression of the Christian imperialism of the Byzantine monarchy" (xi). A further mosaic opposite page 120 illustrates the adoration of the Magi, combining eastern art with styles from the Gothic period.

There are two illustrations of Christian art from Ireland (op. 200) and Anglia (opp. 208), with the first displaying a "magical and fantastic impression" very different from Mediterranean art, and the second showing an example of Irish calligraphy and ornamentation, but not without a southern influence. An illustration from a ninth century manuscript has the emperor Charles the Bald wearing clothing from the Byzantine era that he so longed to emulate (xiii). A relief from the altar of S. Ambrozio in Milan (opp. 232) is a form of Carolingian metal-work that shows two figures paying homage in feudal style to the bishop (xiii). A drawing from the eleventh century illustrates "the conversion of the North" (opp. 248) xiv), dramatizing the medieval emphasis on the divine origin of imperial authority. A golden and purple illumination of a manuscript of Rabanus Maurus (opp. 258) xiv) shows the emperor Louis the Pious in Roman dress as "a type of the Christian soldier." Finally, Emperor Otto III is depicted, early in the eleventh century, receiving the homage of his people (between 280-281), expressed in a combined Germanic and Byzantine style (xiv).

Dawson's work discusses the tensions and the eventual synthesis between Christianity and classical culture, with significant bridges to the north established by Cassiodorus, Boëthius and Benedictine monasticism. Here we see described the growth of a mixed Roman-barbarian culture that began with the early predations of the north into the south, but eventuated in a reverse order with Roman encroachment throughout continental Europe. Early Christian thinkers during the fourth and fifth century invasion periods dreamed of how finally, "by becoming Christians—or rather Catholics—the flood would break itself against the rock of Christ" (93). The monumental event that was seen to fulfill this hope was the conversion of Clovis in 492, although the conversion was also a stage in the struggle between Roman Catholics and Gothic Arians. It was the growing hegemony that would hold the Christian culture together through these "dark ages." This rule would also contribute a distinctive eastern flavor to later northern European religion and culture, including the influence of the growing power of Islam. This power in turn would deeply influence the philosophico-theological synthesis of scholasticism.

The conversion of the barbarians of the north was hindered severely by the power of the Huns, Gepids and Lombards, and even more by the mighty explosion of Islam. This period saw the beginnings of the form of political syncretism that developed between the popes of the fifth and sixth centuries, first the Caesars of the east, then the various sovereigns of the north. However, it also saw the growth of a specific spirituality in the union of Roman Catholic faith with Celtic culture and the influence of this in return upon the tribes of the continent. In the interaction between the Irish and English missionary movements and the peasants of the continent we see early spontaneous syncretistic developments intertwining Christian faith and the nature religions of Europe, about which we shall have more to say directly. For Dawson, however, Christianity did succeed in remoulding the peasant culture, as is shown by the disappearance of the gods and the reconsecration of the holy places, though he admits that all such forms continued to spring up in popular religious practice (203-204).

The seventh century, however, also saw the appearance of a new Anglo-Saxon native culture that would deeply affect developments in Europe, including the development of the Catholic Church (206). There would also be a drive toward the vernacular languages (typified in Cyril and Methodius and later of course in Luther), but still ever in tension with the languages of the Mediterranean. Thus, European reorganization was to come from two sources; "For it was the Anglo-Saxon monks, and, above all, St. Boniface, who first realized that union of Teutonic initiative and Latin order which is the source of the whole medieval development of culture" (213).

The Carolingian Renaissance beginning in the middle of the eighth century syncretized a military idealism with a religious one, destined to become the age of chivalry. Charlemagne would develop the theocratic ideal beyond the Byzantine style and along Teutonic lines, but there would be a far more intensified struggle between Church and State ensuing from this by the end of the first millennium. Out of all this amalgam was growing the twofold syncretistic thrust that we shall study further: the many ordering tendencies of monastic intellectual and cultural preservation as well as the vagaries of popular religiosity. All of these tendencies can be seen in the outgrowth of the conversion of the north during the age of the Vikings. Dawson recognizes here too those seeds of syncretism in the integration of Scandinavian military ideals, the native religions of the peasants, the tutelage of the landowners, all within a tradition that began with the baptism of Harold in 826 (240). This "conversion" did little to halt Viking piracies, however, until the mid-eleventh century.

In the long run, though, the converted Vikings brought a new vitality into Europe, as these peoples became the new "champions of Christendom" (245). This would also produce the kind of syncretistic elements that are evident in one of the symposia on syncretism (Cf. Appendix II). Dawson comments on this development, "The Viking ideal was by itself too destructive and sterile to be capable of producing the higher fruits of culture" (254).

What, then, did produce this higher synthesis? As Dawson recounts, amid all the amalgam of popular religiosity and military power, many intellectual and spiritual reformers came forth out of the Carolingian tradition—Paschasius Radbertus, Bernard of Vienne, Hincmar of Rheims, Ebbo of Rheims. To such as these the beginnings of the struggle of the Church against secular princes can be traced, anticipated by Pope Nicholas I (858-867) heralded by Sylvester II (Gerbert), and leading to the growth of ecclesiastical power beginning with Gregory VII (Hildebrand), and culminating in the influence of Innocent III in the thirteenth century. Out of the confusion then, arose the Church as "the true organ of culture" (269). This was the rise of what H. Richard Niebuhr, in his great modern classic, *Christ and Culture*, (Niebuhr, 1951, Ch. 4), was to call the "Christ above Culture" or "synthetic-centrist" model, with its strengths and its weaknesses. It is the setting for the dynamics beginning with the growth of scholasticism in the eleventh century and its high point with Aquinas in the mid-thirteenth century. It is here that we situate our final observations on the history of the formative European syncretic process, with its tension between spontaneous growth and critical synthesis, to prepare us to develop a theological and pastoral praxis of syncretic process. We must again take note of the Metaxy that bridges primal chaos and ultimate order, as having two distinct but interrelated thrusts—intellectual synthesis and popular syncretism. For the popular element we must backtrack into the earlier periods mentioned above, in order then to examine the scholarly synthesis that began the theological project to which we hope to contribute.

In his recent penetrating study of popular Germanic religiosity, *The Germanization of Early Medieval Christianity*, James Russell has created a set of useful dating brackets: February 2, 992, the date of the coronation of Otto I as Holy Roman Emperor, and October 11, 1962, the date of the opening of the Second Vatican Council—a millennium of European and largely Germanic domination of Christianity (Russell, 1994, vii). Russell's book is a more specifically socioreligious and ethnological study than was Dawson's, but it covers roughly the same time lines. I have chosen it here because of its excellent perception of the syncretism of popular religion during that period, in which Russell seeks to develop "a model of religious interaction between folk-religious societies and universal religions" in the encounter of the Germanic peoples with Christianity (3). This book is especially appropriate for a study of syncretism, since, as Russell writes, "Distinguishing between that which is essential to Christianity and that which may be modified or omitted to advance the process of Christianization, has always been a major problem for the missionary" (11). The consequence of this problem is to walk the path between the opposing dangers of cultural alienation and religious syncretism (understood in its pejorative sense here), unless, as Russell notes, we wish to agree with Emperor Julian (and to some degree Hendrik Kramer) that cultural groups have entirely incompatible religions (12).

Russell suggests, with Durkheim, that Christianity has a better chance of taking root in an "anomic" culture, such as the declining Roman empire of the first two centuries of the common era, than in a culturally homogeneous and stable society, such as that of the Germanic tribes. In the case of the latter, the local religion maintains a greater strength and capacity to absorb the imported Christian symbols and ideas, rather than in a dominance of the existing Christian symbols and practices. This contrast is of deep significance for later missionary activity among the non-European culture groups. It was certainly true that the Germanic tribes, however much their leaders felt attracted by hellenistic culture, had the strength to absorb Roman Christianity rather than to be absorbed by it. There were numerous Frankish or Germanic elements that had the strength to recontextualize Christian meanings or even to divert them into new channels.

To mention only the more significant, there was the dynamistic or animistic mentality of the tribal religion to give "power" to sacred objects like shrines, rocks, graves and the like, and thus deeply affect practices within the liturgy (43ff.). But this was only a more superficial aspect of liturgical alteration. More significantly, the Mass itself became a "good work" as contrasted with a sacrificial meal (180), and the "private mass" began to proliferate, with many missionaries cooperating, in an effort to "accommodate" the Church to the culture and thus redefine Germanic traditions (121). The mass that developed from this tradition, as Jungmann has shown in his various works, was the mass with vastly increased and multiple gestures, prayer with folded hands, the untouchability of sacred vessels except by the priest or deacon, and so forth. Likewise, the strong symbolization of political power within the liturgy manifested the sociopolitical cohesion of the Roman Empire of the German Nation, although this cohesion already had precedent in Byzantine Catholicism (171).

In the area of ethics, the powerful warrior codes of the Germans would deeply alter, not only the very image of Christ himself, but of Christian values in general (124), Russell calls the tenth century the period of "the Ottonian captivity of the Church," which would affect social ethics profoundly (124). This period transformed much of the "world-rejecting," eschatological spirit of hellenistic Platonism into a "world-accepting," cyclical mentality of tribal life. While it may be that Russell overstates here the "world-denying" side to hellenistic Christianity (certain aspects of Graeco-Roman culture hardly being world-denying), he makes his point in relation to the feudal system that would absorb the (ideally) transcendent Christian ethic and place even Church hierarchy within the solidarity system called *comitatus* (126). One could also note the negative side of all this—that the system of vassalage built on kin-groupings contributed to the nepotism that so deeply affected the medieval Church (129).

Russell details the "world-accepting" "Germanic beatitudes" that stood over against those of Jesus: the value of wealth, glory, strength, honor, family connections, and even vengeance. (120-122) The missionaries from Rome as well as from Britain strove to redefine these values by merging them with the ambivalent code of chivalry, in a movement that peaked with the Crusades. This powerful "heroic" culture shaped the popular image of Christ and made him into more a "warrior-hero," and (though Russell does not mention this), may also have influenced the development of "the just war" theory that defended the right and duty to fight in order to save nation, family or Church. In general, Russell has vividly described the complexities of this association between the warrior culture and Roman Christianity.

Doctrinal issues as well would arise from popular syncretism. One of the greatest was that of Arianism, which Russell sees as strengthened in the north by Germanic ideas of hierarchy and subordination. Soteriology and Christology took a dramatic turn in the form of Anselm's use of the satisfaction theory (already developed in Roman society, of course) according to the *Wergild* practice of redeeming a person at a price (171). Ecclesiology, though, one should add, was deeply affected by Germanic syncretism. For one thing, in Germanic society there was no "separation of church and state," (139) as, I would add, there is no such separation in any tribal society; values in general are immanent rather than transcendent.

The power of the Germanic kings figures prominently in this history, since it combines the words for sacred king *reiks* with the word *theudans* (tribal chief), as in "Theodoric" (174). This would explain, of course, how and why Theodoric might put to death so revered a figure as Boëthius, because he represented a rival culture as well as a rival theology. While in essence this royal encroachment on ecclesiastical authority might seem little different from Graeco-Roman caesaropapism, its application in the north would create a system still more distant from the Roman center. Thus developed the practice of the *Eigenkirche*, or proprietary church, controlled locally by feudal lords. Hence the momentous investiture controversy that would dominate ecclesiastical and secular politics from the eleventh through the twelfth centuries and maintain some sway until the Enlightenment.

One discerns in this brief collection of historical examples only a hint of the elements that would be addressed by the Council (Vatican II) that convened at the end of what Russell calls the Germanic era. As with all instances of syncretic process, those of a "progressive" or reforming mentality will always be well advised to tread lightly in imputing blame for "abuses" in the Church, as was done in an all too facile way by theologians immediately following the Council. A careful examination of history always reveals good reasons why certain forces were released in church and society, and why any attempts at revisioning must take all factors into account. The investigator also does well to try to understand how a more reflective "rationalization" of syncretic processes tries to cope with such an amalgam as emerged out of the "dark ages" into the period of the high middle ages. Hence, before ending the present chapter, we must examine, again in broad strokes, the efforts at intellectual synthesis that accompanied the popular syncretism of the middle ages. Indeed, the synthesis-syncretism tension is paradigmatic for the examination of the interaction of faith and culture throughout the remainder of this book.

THE RATIONAL SYNTHESIS

There is no pretense here of entering into a vast investigation of the Christian medieval synthesis. But the project of any study of the syncretic process demands that one in some way try to recapitulate the labors of the apologists and the early fathers, as we described above, to integrate faith, reason and culture, and thus to develop a more refined method of discernment of the process. Within the enormous output of historical work by the great Étienne Gilson, is one large volume that may serve to guide us in this discussion. I refer to his *History of Christian Philosophy in the Middle Ages*. It is significant that, returning to this book for the first time since my earlier philosophical formation, I found his early chapters devoted to the labors of these very fathers of whom I have written, from the apologists to the Cappadocians.

I should also note of Gilson a point often overlooked by some neo-scholastics who tended to treat "faith and reason" as entirely separate categories, that Gilson (following Aquinas) always recognized the priority of faith and revelation. (See his introduction (Gilson, 1955, 3-6) That Gilson himself never gave in to this dichotomy gives us an example of one who, within the synthesis, recognized revelation as a criterion. He writes,

> If the essence of the Christian message had been "corrupted" into a philosophy as early as the second century, Christianity would have soon ceased to exist as a religion and, consequently, there could be no history of Christian philosophy to relate. In point of fact, it is not philosophy that kept Christianity alive during fourteen centuries, rather it is Christianity that did not allow philosophy to perish (Gilson, 1955,6).

In this succinct analysis lies the key to authentic syncretic process.

Beyond these theologians, Gilson also discusses especially the work of Augustine, Victorinus, Boëthius, Cassiodorus and Gregory the Great. We shall not detain ourselves on these figures, beyond pointing out how each of them and their lesser contemporaries strove for some kind of order and synthesis. Augustine especially sought to construct a Christian theology of history and Boëthius and Cassiodorus to collect all things knowable and to order them within the culture of northern Europe. Learning from such thinkers as these, we must continue to search out authentic criteria for the true Christian synthesis that reached a summit with Aquinas and began its decline shortly after his death.

In the person of John Scotus Erigena, the ninth century synthetic genius, the quest for a Christian synthesis finds the kind of encyclopedist who seeks to integrate the biblical doctrines of creation and revelation with a philosophy of nature by way of Greek metaphysics, culminating (not unlike in the thought of Teilhard de Chardin) in the victory of Christ. Like Teilhard, Erigena came upon hard times with his contemporaries, who apparently could not embrace this "barbarian, placed on the outskirts of the world" (127), who so scandalized the "sober teachings of the Latin tradition" (128). It was a movement that did not survive him, but his career serves as a sign that "barbarians" were now involved in the syncretic process.

This historical process, as Gilson describes it, passes through the Carolingian renaissance and its decadence, and draws us into the Benedictine monasticism that survived it and in which its higher achievements flourished. The philosophico-theological apex of monasticism is typified in the eleventh century labors of Anselm of Canterbury. Gilson, seeking a Christian philosophy rather than a discussion of "revealed truth," bypasses Anselm's massive *Cur Deus Homo?*, and dwells on his *Proslogion* and *Monologion*, on Anselm's efforts to construct a harmony of faith and reason focused on demonstrating the existence of God. This is itself a vast field of endeavor involving both philosophers and theologians, with Karl Barth and Bernard Lonergan being among the most prominent. For Gilson, Anselm is justifiably called by some the father of scholasticism: he inaugurated a "science of faith" that would henceforth strive to keep faith and culture within a tensive harmony (139).

After Anselm, a story that touches deeply on the tensive relationship between faith and culture is the stormy and in many ways pathetic one of Peter Abelard. Within our theme, Abelard is of importance for two reasons. First, he moved reflection forward into the famous scholastic format called *Sic et Non*, which strove to establish a civilized way of dealing with difference—with the dialectic of opposites seeking a synthesis. But secondly, Abelard was also a rightful heir of Justin and Clement of Alexandria in his search for "believers" who were outside of Christianity. Hence, those prior to (and even after) Christ who followed the philosophical quest for truth were for Abelard "gentiles by nation but not by faith" (162-163). Gilson could say of him, "Abelard had a clear mind and a generous heart. Christian revelation was never for him an impassible barrier dividing the chosen from the condemned and truth from error" (163). His influence was momentous, and in our tensive Metaxy he symbolizes the quest for order grounded not only in reason but in love.

In order to pursue his search for Christian philosophy, Gilson interrupts his journey through Christian territory and detours, if that is not too negative a metaphor, through the vast territory of the Jewish and Muslim philosophers, again significantly for the sake of what we are calling syncretic process. To begin with, Muslims involved in philosophical speculation were, like their Christian counterparts, believers in a positive revelation, seeking to order their thought rationally, by turning basically to Aristotle, and through him to aspects of Platonism. One can imagine the fundamentalist contemporaries of the great Arab thinkers crying "Syncretism!" Gilson writes, "Like Christian faith, Islamic faith soon felt the need of an intellectual interpretation, be it only to correct the literal interpretation of the Koran upheld by the fundamentalists of those times" (182). Those endeavors did not, of course, end there, since it was through the Arabs that Aristotle and Plato came to be disseminated throughout Europe.

Without detaining ourselves on the specific ideas and questions asked by such as Alfarabi, Avicenna and Averroes, it is worth our effort to examine the attention that Gilson gives to Avicenna, the genius whose project resembles that of Erigena. Avicenna too sought to integrate all knowledge—logic, physics (as understood by Aristotle, and thus a "cosmology"), astronomy, psychology (what scholastics came to call "rational psychology" and eventually "philosophy of human nature"), metaphysics and finally theology. Avicenna seems to have used reason more as his starting point than revelation, but he

was clearly attempting to demonstrate whatever can be demonstrated
to support the teachings of Mohammed, such as the resurrection.
Averroes too constructed a similar synthesis, and joins Avicenna in
the ranks of those exploring the Metaxy for a key to unity and order
amid so much disorder and chaos.

Among Jewish philosophers, the name of Moses Maimonides most
enriches the cultural synthesis of the middle ages. He too highlights
the place of Aristotle in his metaphysical contribution to a rationale
for religious faith, and benefits, as would Aquinas, from the labors of
the Arabs. Gilson notes, however, that Maimonides disagreed with
the Muslims in their claim to have found a "philosophical" argument
for religious truths, and agreed more with Thomas that rational arguments simply serve to show a certain human cohesiveness to the
work of theology and the truths of revelation (231).

The medieval universities represent the theological-cultural synthesis, with theology holding the primacy of place among the facul-
ties of theology, law, medicine and arts. This is certainly one of the
foremost examples of the "Christ above culture" model of Niebuhr.
The fact that the university gradually passed from Church to national ownership is an indication of the growing culture of
Christendom, with the complexities this would present for the future of the syncretic process. But in the thirteenth century the theologians of the universities, such as Grosseteste and Bacon of Oxford,
and Albert of Paris represent the effort to spread Christian truth
through secular learning, including a synthesis of secular sciences
such as biology with theological thought.

Albert, the great Dominican who was also Aquinas's teacher, was a
giant in the history of synthetic learning. In Albert one detects a clue
to the Christian quest for criteria on how to synthesize faith and
secular knowledge without falling into uncritical syncretism. Thus,
as Gilson recognizes, the movement toward "theological syncretism"
(xi) under Greek and Arabian influence, came upon hard times, especially with the inclusion of Aristotle being roundly forbidden by
bishops in the early thirteenth century and again after Thomas's death
in 1274. This too is significant if we recall the more balanced response of Bartolomé de Las Casas, two centuries later, trained in
scholasticism and Aristotelian philosophy. Las Casas, without totally

rejecting Aristotle, was to radically relativize his work when "the Philosopher" espoused false ethical teachings about the inequality of human beings and "natural slavery." To the extent that Aristotle held sway over Christian theology and ethics in this area, one may argue that, under the guise of "synthesis," a more spontaneous and ill-conceived racist form of syncretism had developed (See Hanke, 1959, 1979). The historical syncretic process would in this case be submitted to intense scrutiny by the Church some two centuries after the high medieval period.

Albert established two significant positions in dealing with the tension between philosophy and Christian theology. First, he asserted that theologians must thoroughly master the thought of the Greek-Arab world, different as it was from that of the Fathers. Secondly, however, Albert left the legacy of a transmitter of philosophical and natural knowledge without attempting to synthesize it creatively. He sought "real scientific knowledge"—a knowledge not of words and subtle distinctions, but of "things" (Gilson, 1957, 279). In a sense, Albert may be called a predecessor of the kind of phenomenological methodology that is so necessary as a stage in the process of understanding another culture and faith.

Albert's close contemporary, Roger Bacon, also utilized the work of Aristotle through the Arabs, especially Avicenna, in the study of metaphysics, the philosophy of human nature, and "natural theology." Bacon did not intend to create an exposition of Christian wisdom, but simply to urge the pursuit of research, and especially of experimentation. This search for "concrete" evidence led Gilson to say of him that his very errors often show a mind ahead of its time. This "unhappy genius," as Gilson calls him, (312) alone among thirteenth century thinkers, dreamed of a republic of Christians, united under the popes, and directed by the truth of a comprehensive Christian wisdom. Although one should exercise some "suspicion" about the potential "Christendom" character of this aspiration, it is a high example of a metaxic hope to establish order in history.

Within "the Golden Age of Scholasticism," we need address here only the two great figures of Bonaventure and Thomas Aquinas. The labors of Bonaventure, in one aspect, anticipate the work of Bernard Lonergan, by establishing love as the connecting link between reason and faith, Bonaventure's doctrine being characterized by his famous phrase, "the itinerary of the soul toward God" (Gilson, 1959, 332). Bonaventure contributed a synthesis of the philosophical language of Aristotle and the doctrinal teaching of Augustine. This synthesis would produce later great Franciscan contributors like Duns Scotus and Ramon Lull, the latter being not only a scholar but a courageous and tireless missionary. He was a seeker after both the evangelization of and dialogue with the Muslims, which was to lead to his violent death as an old man (700). This was a testimony to the Metaxy sealed by martyrdom (see Reilly, 1978, 70-74,117-132).

Thomas Aquinas crowns the Golden Age of Scholasticism in his incorporation of Augustine and Aristotle, though with an emphasis opposite (but not contradictory) to that of Bonaventure. His quest for a unity of philosophy and theology provides a further criterion for the syncretic process, a desire to depict a rational understanding of the world in the light of the gospel. Thomas's career manifests the same desire as shown by earlier scholastics to achieve order and interpretation within all the multiplicity around him. His emphasis was, as is well known, on the intellect rather than on the will, so that his transformation of epistemology and philosophy of human nature was shown especially in his identification of the "substantial form" of the human person with the human soul. Another sign of his genius was his famous intuition of the pure act of being as ultimately the "nature" of God and in a derived way as constituting the uniqueness of the human person. We should not forget, however, that Aquinas was not only a philosophical theologian but a prolific biblical exegete as well as a political theorist and ethicist. All of these elements helped to constitute his contribution to a synthesis of faith and culture within what we are calling the syncretic process.

This brings to a completion our brief summary of the medieval European syncretic process, both in its spontaneous syncretism and its scholarly synthesis. However, we should not totally neglect the period of disintegration of the scholastic synthesis in the fourteenth century, if for no other reason than that this leads us into what Gilson called "The Modern Way" (Gilson, 1957 Part 11). In William of Ockham we meet a scholar who tired of the later scholastics' sterile repetition of earlier formulae and their fruitless speculations. His fa-

mous "razor," applied to the absurdities of multiple "universals," is
the instrument of the "nominalism" later attributed to him, not without justification.

Quite rightly seeking to purify Christian thought of sterile speculation, and thus witnessing strongly to the primacy of faith, Ockham
also helped to destroy the synthesis of faith and reason desired by
earlier scholasticism. Ockham's influence on Martin Luther, by way
of Gabriel Biel and the University of Erfurt, displays further the irony
of the syncretic process for Christians. The many needed reforms,
including that of biblical studies, represented especially with Luther
but also Wycliffe and Tyndale, are a positive contribution to Christian history. Likewise, Ockham's political positions, especially his "razor" as applied to the separation of spiritual and temporal powers,
further influenced the more radical thought of Marsilius of Padua,
both an Ockhamist and an Averroist in his separation of faith and
reason. All of this history was to leave a legacy to be realized, from
the Catholic side at least, in the work of the Second Vatican Council,
especially on religious freedom and the due recognition of a certain
autonomy of secular culture (see Marsilius of Padua, 1980, *passim*).

This being said, however, Ockham also left a legacy of antithesis
rather than synthesis. The fact that Protestant and Catholic reforma-
tions wound up going their separate ways and even becoming counter-
movements is the tragic dimension of this breakup of the synthesis.
A further aspect of the dichotomies highlighted by Ockham touches
directly on the theme of the present book, and is symbolized by the
events, cited in the opening chapter, that further divided Protestant
Christians in the seventeenth century and led to the accusatory use
of the word "syncretism." As a consequence, all of us today, Catholic
and Protestant alike, who seek for not only interchurch unity, but a
unity of culture within the Christian faith, find ourselves confronted
with a challenge to try to synthesize all these "*disjecta membra*," more
radically separated now than at the close of the "dark ages."

The two chapters to follow, then, constitute a unity: that is, they
are constructed on the basis of the principle that all theology is "practical," although not necessarily usable in all contexts. I can make this
assertion only after more than a quarter of a century as both missionary and academic, having lived amid the "theological messiness"

(Starkloff, 1994, 93) of a highly syncretistic and at times "compart-mentalized" or "dual system" context. For perhaps an indefinite pe-riod, in our work among aboriginal peoples especially (but no doubt in the wider society), we must be content to live in patience with syncretism as a process of what I am calling the Metaxy. The concept of Metaxy is important here, certainly for Catholics but very likely for all mainstream Christians, because church leadership is always exceedingly uncomfortable with the idea of Metaxy—of a time of tension during which issues of doctrine are not "settled once and for all." The Church, to employ a famous term from the Myers-Briggs vocabulary, is an excruciatingly "J" personality: that is, it longs for "closure," but the syncretic process does not lend itself to easy clo-sure. This fact has led me to compose, in the following chapters, not a complete systematic theology, but a methodological framework both for a systematics and for pastoral procedure.

In the remaining two chapters, I shall first attempt to construct a methodology that offers criteria for a creative encounter with syncre-tism. With that background, I shall address "cases" for applying the criteria that we have established. At the risk of sounding pretentious, I suggest that we who "do theology" in syncretistic contexts share a deep community with the great thinkers and doers whose work we have surveyed thus far. Standing on the shoulders of such giants, and benefitting from both their successes and their mistakes, we may hope to use our view of the space behind us to pick out a sound terrain for moving forward.

2

TOWARD A THEOLOGY OF THE IN-BETWEEN

To this point, we have followed the labors of thinkers, from the early apologists to the twentieth century, in their efforts to take seriously the principle of the Incarnation, to enflesh the Word within culture. We have barely entered, however, into the epoch of the "World Church" that Rahner saw coming to birth at the Second Vatican Council. The theologians of the late twentieth century have begun to address this gospel mandate, as we have seen at the conclusion of the last chapter. It is our task to accompany them now as we begin to construct a systematic approach to a theology of the Metaxy, of the "In Between," where faith and culture interact, both to contend and to complement each other, and to join in a higher synthesis.

THE PHILOSOPHY OF THE IN-BETWEEN:

AN INTERPRETIVE KEY

We cannot here enter into the vast five-volume project of Eric Voegelin, a passionate quest interrupted only by his death, to explore the universal quest for meaning and order in history. But the Metaxy that possessed him so passionately can again be employed at this point. Granted, Voegelin's pilgrimage is now inadequate for the needs of a world Church, because of its almost total emphasis on the "western civilization" that emerged from the biblical world and entered into that of the Graeco-Romans. But incomplete as this work is, it is a formidable instrument for expressing the great gift to the western world of "historical consciousness." Within Voegelin's Metaxy, the phenomenon of syncretism carries within it a potential to enhance

the power of interpretation, representing as it does the longing for
unity amid diversity.

Voegelin's primary concern was that of the political philosopher
seeking the true *polis*, the integrated human city. But from the outset
this quest was an ardently religious one, because Voegelin perceived
the deeply spiritual nature of struggles of the Metaxy, as we see in his
first volume when he recognizes the significance of the encounter
between the Syrian High God and the Lord God of Israel as a syncretistic one (Voegelin, 1958, 273). Finally, however, we find our point
of departure in his last volume, *In Search of Order*, where, at the outset, Voegelin alludes implicitly to the Platonic and New Testament
concept *koinonia* (Voegelin, 1957, 36 and *passim*), or participatory
existence in the Metaxy, where the divine and the human meet. It
seems to be only at the later stage of his journey that Voegelin tried
to develop an actual theory of the Metaxy, although it appears earlier
in his identification of the Resurrection as the paradigmatic "event"
that constitutes meaning in the total historical process (Voegelin,
1974, 243).

In this final volume, Voegelin does move toward further clarification of the In-Between:

> The metaxy, then, remains the symbol that validly expresses the
> experience of existence in the Between of thing-reality, including
> the bodily location of consciousness and of Beyond-reality, but
> certain ramifications of its meaning we discovered when the
> Beyond becomes more clearly differentiated (Voegelin, 1987,30).

This is a typical case of Voegelinian density, but it contains deep
significance: to put things more concretely, like St. Paul, this philosopher was "groaning in the body" while seeking the vision of Eternity. So Voegelin chose rather to *embrace* the tension as he saw it
embraced by Plato as well as by the book of Genesis. The tension of
the In-Between is thus a perpetual intellectual and spiritual combat
as humankind struggles to understand the meaning of the Cosmos
(Voegelin, 1987, 83). Thus could he understand the intensity with
which Plato interpreted the mystery of the Beyond and its Parousia:
"The experiences of divine, formative presence are events in the metaxy
of existence, and the symbols engendered by the Parousia express

divine reality as an irruption of ordering force from the Beyond into the existential struggle for order" (97). One can readily sympathize with Voegelin's passion for the discovery of order in history, and thus tolerate the sometimes baffling mental gymnastics he engages in for this quest—one that at times seems almost to unhinge his mind. Fortunately, there are other scholars critically sympathetic with Voegelin to assist us in clarifying his meaning in the use of the concept of the Metaxy. Thus, the Old Testament scholar Bernhard Anderson supports his endeavor to unite theology and politics (Anderson, 1978, 62-100). "The heart of the problem," according to Anderson, is what Voegelin called Israel's "mortgage" within the Metaxy, that is its identity as "the Chosen People." Voegelin had also identified the Greek mortgage on history as its search for the *polis* (Voegelin, 1957, 263). To unpack this metaphor, what is intended here is that each culture must eventually pay off its responsibility to social order by redeeming it under some historical form. Philosophy thus joins with the Old Testament in the effort to illuminate the mystery of existence; another commentator calls this the "metaxic structure" of "the question" (Wiser, 1978, 127-138, at 134).

Another author, while faulting Voegelin's lack of a sense of the gospel as salvation, highlights how the process by which the "gospel myth" had to merge with Greek philosophy in order to permeate the hellenistic world of its time (Douglas, 1978, 139-154, at 140). This had to occur especially in unison with the rejection of gnosticism, with its attempt to free itself from the tensions of the In-Between through an escape into the realm of salvation from historical existence in this world (154). Another friendly critic of Voegelin's, Robert Doran, understands how the Metaxy awakens "the primordial experience of existence" that keeps alive the tension against any false lulling to sleep of resistance to imperialism or totalitarianism (Doran, 1990, 520). As we shall see, the syncretic process is often the instrument by which historical meaning can be continued or retrieved by means of the arduous labor of obedience to the Word of God joined to respect for human cultural traditions.

Yet another Voegelin commentator locates the great scholar's Metaxy within the dizzying realm between the ancient Anaxamander and later Greek philosophy—the "in-between consciousness wherein humanity becomes luminous to itself through both the struggles of the individual awareness and the communication with all other units of consciousness" (Corrington, 1978, 155-195, at 167). This author quotes Voegelin himself: "The mankind whose humanity unfolds in the flux of presence is universal mankind. The irreversibility of mankind is constituted by the divine process in the metaxy" (Voegelin, 1978, 304).

Since our theology in this book aims at creative responses to pastoral concerns, what are we to do with the combined vertiginous height and menacing depth of Voegelin's thought? Well, at the very beginning of our systematic interpretation we must renounce any expectation that the Metaxy will be transcended within history (Corrington, 1978, 187). Thus, as a movement within the Metaxy, the syncretic process by its nature will find its complete resolution only at the Parousia. This is not only a theological response but a deeply spiritual one: with Moltmann, we can embrace such a struggle authentically only through hope. However, theology stands to be enriched by this process if it envisions it as "drama," enacted through a "ritual process." To understand how this occurs we must move from the philosophy of history to the discipline of cultural anthropology, especially as developed by Victor and Edith Turner.

The work of the Turners is of special value in the matter of syncretism because it both sketches out a phenomenology of process and is in the final analysis "theological." While this spouse-team strove to focus on the "scientific" study of cultural dynamics, their own Christian faith led them do undertake one study of ritual process that helps make their work valuable for discerning the role of syncretic processes. Indeed, their work will help us to focus more particularly on the struggles of "marginalized peoples," which is, as Schreiter and Siller have also observed, a major concern for any study of syncretism within missiology (see Siller, 1991, 9-10; Schreiter, 1985,152-158). As André Droogers shrewdly observed, on the process of social and religious renewal, the "margins" of society are of vital importance, and Victor Turner has taken the lead in interpreting this process (Droogers, 1989, 19). Likewise, David Carrasco, describing a context that typifies such struggles, notes, "The complex process by which rituals, beliefs and symbols from different religions are combined into new meanings, syncretism is most clearly represented in ritual performances that enable people to locate themselves within the new world of meaning" (Carrasco, 1990, 169).

Victor Turner's early field research as a cultural anthropologist took place in southern Africa, especially in Zambia, where he studied the "rites of passage" among the Ndembu people (See V. Turner, 1967). His findings confirmed the theories a half century earlier of Arnold van Gennep (Van Gennep, 1908), who originated the dynamic triad that Turner was to employ in all of his work. Rituals involving birth, initiations, marriage, entrance into societies or trades, and finally death—indeed just about every ritual expression, involved this triad. That is, all candidates undergoing such rites pass through three stages: separation from the ordinary life of the community, a stage of marginalization or "liminality" (a "threshold" existence), and finally reintegration into the life of the community. Turner first focused especially on the rites of male circumcision and their role in facilitating the passage of boys into responsible adult manhood.

Turner's later book, *The Ritual Process* (Turner, 1995), had as its central field study the rites by which a seemingly barren woman's "underperformance" as a child-bearer could be cured, as well as on another rite for correcting "overperformance" in a woman who has borne twins, since twins were also seen as a result of some form of witchery in a society with no sources of milk. In this book, Turner began to develop his theory that these rites are not merely local ceremonies but are also archetypal for a fundamental need in society— the dynamic passage from one stage of life to a better one. He eventually argued that all of human society is in such a process, which it ritualizes either consciously or unconsciously. He turned, for example, to the rites of profession in monasteries, and beyond these to the self-chosen marginalization of St. Francis of Assisi and his early followers. In this history he found his triad confirmed: Francis's earliest movement was just such a liminal "performance" aimed at his own renewal of himself and eventually that of his first companions. It rapidly developed into a corrective symbol for the Church as a whole. But Turner also pointed out that the Franciscans were unable to perpetuate their liminal condition for long, and that it was a perfectly natural process that they would in some ways resume a more stable position within society and church (Turner, 1995, 140-153). Turner went on to publish a large corpus of work that argued for the creative process of liminality in society.

At this point I simply reduce the examination of Turner's work to the themes of syncretic process, although elsewhere I have developed implications for ecclesiology and mission (Starkloff, 1997, 643-668). Turner went on, especially in *The Ritual Process*, to develop two further categories: these were "structure" and "communitas." The first is a word used to describe the organized society in which people live their day-do-day existence, while the second denotes the intimate shared life experienced by those who are "liminalized." That is, in passage rituals, the initiands are kept together in a tight group and watched over by special adepts until they are reintegrated into the larger whole. This kind of existence Turner also calls "anti-structure," to indicate the fact that such a state is not ordered at all like daily social life, and may even seem chaotic to ordinary eyes (see Turner 1967, 97ff. and 1995, 125 ff.).

Turner's theory seen in this way is an optimistic one, which argues that society has means built into it which help it to keep revitalizing itself by means of the creativity exercised on the margins. Thus he later applied his ideas to such "social dramas" as revolutions and religious resistance to tyranny. A new slant to the theory of marginality emerges here, in another of his books, *Dramas, Fields and Metaphors*, where he argues that all social dynamics have the nature of "dramas" or "social performances." That is, people instinctively act out their social tensions in the fashion of an orchestrated "moving action" called drama (Turner, 1974).

Still later, Turner teamed up with his wife Edith to study the phenomenon of the pilgrimage as another case of voluntary liminality that functions to renew the life of the Church. Examples are the famous pilgrimages such as Lough Derg in Ireland, Guadalupe in Mexico, and LaSallette and Lourdes in France. They view pilgrimages as manifesting all the elements of liminality, especially in their potential for renewing the life of the Church. From here Turner would go on to develop his ideas into theories of play and more "anthropology of performance," demonstrating how passage processes become factors in social action or at least in helping permanently marginalized persons find "communitas" or belonging (Turner, 1982). He was especially fascinated by the highly syncretistic ritual of Candomble, the ceremony of many of the marginalized peoples of Brazil (Turner, 1988, 47-71).

What, to get more precise, does the methodology of the Turners contribute to our investigation of syncretic process? Recent studies that have tried to empathize with syncretism show how syncretic processes facilitate a retention or recovery of cultural identity among the "threatened" cultures under attack by more dominant cultures. Syncretism becomes for the imperiled and marginalized culture a solution to their problem, while it represents a threat for the culture that is attempting to impose itself holus bolus on another. In the final chapter, we shall examine pastoral cases of such syncretism, but here we probe more deeply into Turner's theory in its deeper implications, especially in how it touches on ecclesiology, and how the Church might more critically and sympathetically facilitate such syncretism as a process on the way to synthesis.

Every culture articulates itself through metaphors, and one of these is, says Turner, the metaphor of ritual process and liminality. In other words, human social life finds its image in ritual that symbolizes the triadic process of separation, liminality and reintegration. At various points, of course, this process may become conflictual or at least tensive, such as when a culture is under threat, and finds ways to ritualize the mediation or elimination of the threat, as in the cases of those threatened and syncretizing cultures discussed by Boff. In cases like this, the culture generates anti-structural processes in the form of symbolic actions. Thus, Turner writes, "The components of what I have called anti-structure, such as communitas and liminality, are the conditions for the production of root metaphors, conceptual archetypes, paradigms, models for, and the rest" (Turner, 1974, 50). When a culture enters into such a process it is moving in a dramatic mode, a mode of performance: "Social dramas, then, are units of aharmonic or disharmonic process, arising in conflict situations" (37).

In a sense, then, any culture undergoing such a process is to that extent on a "pilgrimage" (which, I might note, is itself a syncretic phenomenon). As the Turner's wrote, "Liminality is now seen to apply to all phases of decisive cultural change, in which previous orderings of thought and behavior are subject to revision and criticism, where hitherto unprecedented modes of ordering relations between ideas and people become possible and desirable (V. and E. Turner, 1978,2). Such a phenomenon explains why representatives of a dominant culture or of an organized Church can become so agitated over any hint of syncretism, which threatens their accepted version of fidelity to tradition. This leads the Turners to refer to all manifestations of communitas as potentially "subversive" (32).

And yet, such situations are, while potentially dangerous to a society, the source of creative development of the society: "Liminality, marginality, and structural inferiority are conditions in which are frequently generated myths, symbols, rituals, philosophical systems and works of art" (Turner, 1995, 128). It is not gratuitous here to observe that Turner could be describing the Christian Church itself, not only in its earliest tensive situations, but at all points in its history. Indeed, pilgrimages that began as a threat, such as Guadalupe or Lourdes, end by receiving the official blessing of the Church as instruments of its self-recreation. The same can be said of individuals or groups suspected of heresy or schism at a given time. This is not to defend an uncritical embracing of all liminal movements, but simply to point out a fundamental principle in the interpretation of syncretism: such movements often do wind up serving a dynamic process toward a higher integration within the Church. J.A. Möhler, while in no way countenancing heresy, observed how the process of sorting out heresy from orthodoxy is a creative one for the Church (Möhler, 1996, 298-300).

From Turner's treatment of ritual process and its tensions on various "microcosmic" levels, it is no fantastic leap to return to the massive sweep of Eric Voegelin in his preoccupation with the Metaxy on the "macrocosmic" level. The human passion for order in history drives humankind's pilgrimage from its darker origins all the way to its full realization of meaning in the eschatological vision. The one great pilgrimage is the Metaxy on the grand scale, but it plays itself out through the many "in-between" tensions within the histories of different cultures and societies, as well as in the Church. But in fact, all communities have to struggle to find or to re-interpret its meaning for them as they move through history. Is there any essential difference between the Greeks striving to pay off their "mortgage" to history through their quest for the ideal "city," and the many tribal societies today fighting to re-appropriate their identities as "The People"? Let Turner's words conclude this discussion: "Society is a process, a process of adaptation that can never be completely consummated since it involves as many specialized adaptations as there are specialized influences in the environment to be met, as Herbert Spencer wrote a century ago" (Turner, 1967, 271).

TOWARD A THEOLOGICAL METHOD

We are now at the point where we become aware of the need for a systematic theological methodology. Nowhere, I believe, does the interdependence between anthropology, philosophy and theology manifest itself more dramatically than in this discussion. The categories of Voegelin and Turner furnish theology with a dynamic context in which to operate, but it remains for us to create a compatible systematic method to interact with the historical processes we have described.

Any method must be structured to mediate between two poles of the "contest" between syncretism and the Christian tradition. At one pole resides any people's traditional religio-cultural identity, and at the other is the formulation of the faith they have received from the European Church that proclaimed the message to them. How this is to be formulated is the purpose of theological method. How are the creators of a "local theology" to maintain all the life-giving aspects of traditional religiosity, while maintaining fidelity to authentic Christian tradition? How are they to resist movements analogous to early gnosticisms that simply altered Christianity to make of it a tool for their own world-views? Local theologians must first attend to the interrelationships of local symbols and the basic Christian "hierarchy of truths." Secondly, they must follow the *lex orandi lex credendi* principle that evaluates true "Christian performance" in worship that respects the value of the local symbols. Thirdly, theology must examine the "pragmatic," or better, the "praxis" dimension by evaluating how its themes are played out within the life of the community. Fourthly, there must be a method by which the principle of communion in dialogue and collaboration takes place among the churches, and between the churches and the local cultures. Finally, theology must be open to challenges coming from all the churches, and thus avoid any community's turning in upon itself. In what follows we shall be exploring the methodology of Bernard Lonergan as one that can lead us to a creative application of the principles by which our early forebears discerned their passage to an authentic synthesis.

THE METHODOLOGY OF BERNARD LONERGAN

TRANSCENDENTAL PRECEPTS

Throughout the dense, seemingly so "cerebral" writing of Lonergan, there is a dominating passion—the desire to know and understand with integrity and authenticity. For our purposes here, we can concentrate for the most part on his later work *Method in Theology*, to which we turn first for an understanding of the "transcendental precepts" that demand a manifold conversion. Following that discussion, we shall move to an application of Lonergan's now famous "eight functional specialties" for doing theology, asking how local theologians, working in collaboration with the Christian tradition, might negotiate a "passage" through the "liminality" of the tensive Metaxy in quest of order and deeper meaning. We seek, again, a method, which Lonergan describes thusly: "A method is a normative pattern of recurrent and related operations yielding cumulative and progressive results" (Lonergan, 1972, 4).

The theologian who follows this method must be a constantly "converting" person, one who observes the transcendental precepts for surmounting one's own biases in quest of truth and meaning. That is, the theologian must be attentive, intelligent, reasonable and responsible. He or she must practice the kind of attention that cuts through peripheral objects to the object deserving of central focus. Lonergan would have appreciated the work of the American psychologist Csikszentmihalyi on "attention"—the psychic energy employed in selecting what is truly relevant about an experience, and in discarding elements that are merely "distractions."[1] He would appreciate even more how that author recognized Ignatius Loyola's gift for

---

1. I have proposed this approach as part of a means for achieving understanding between cultures. (See Starkloff, 1993, 131)

disciplined organization. He would support the way in which the method of attention resonates with the "Presupposing" to the Ignatian Exercises, which demands an attentive openness to the message of another.

The commandment to "be intelligent" is hardly a mere scolding admonition not to be stupid! It is rather a summation of all the processes by which one arrives at understanding or insight. Even though Lonergan himself was critical of the phenomenological method, all of his writing indicates that he would appreciate Van der Leeuw's use of this method in order to practice attention and remain open to understanding (Van der Leeuw, 1963, Cc. 109-110). By following the phenomenological method in the study of religion, the investigator practices the *epoché*, the unified act both of self-restraint and passionate focusing that the Greek word connotes. For Van der Leeuw, there was no contradiction between one's having a faith and still practicing "intellectual suspense" in order to avoid premature judgment about any religious phenomenon (683). By practicing the discipline of attention, the theologian is enabled to move toward authentic insights into the object of attention.

When Lonergan prescribes reasonableness, he is demanding authenticity of the theologian, the accomplishing of valid judgments about Being and about the role of faith in knowing it. Only by means of judgment can one advance in the realm of morality, faith, justice and commitment. Through attentiveness, intelligence and reason, one is enabled more deeply to understand the "intentionality" of others and to avoid the kind of harsh judgments implied in a too-ready denunciation (Lonergan, 1972, 340-347).

To be responsible in Lonergan's methodology is to know how to "respond" rather than "react." It is the quality essential to "being in love" in relation to the human Other and the eternal Other (33 and Index). By following the precept, really a fifth transcendental precept, one is summing up all the others: to respond out of love. Although he does not seem to have read it, Lonergan would have embraced H. R. Niebuhr's understanding of "responsibility": the freedom from domination by inherited images, after the supreme example of Jesus, our "symbolic form of responsibility" (H.R. Niebuhr, 1978, 154-159). Such freedom, far from *discarding* traditional symbols and teachings, finds new life in their historical unfolding. As applied to a theology of syncretism, responsibility enables the theologian to envision a more deeply inculturated Christianity. In sum, the overall process of the transcendental precepts leads toward "cumulative and progressive results."

CONVERSION

Corresponding to the transcendental precepts, or better, accompanying them, is the multi-faceted experience of conversion as transformation of the knowing subject—in this case the theologian (Lonergan, 1972, 237-244; Index). We shall see below how conversion is the foundational reality of the fifth functional specialty. But for Lonergan conversion must accompany the theologian along every stage of the journey, lest one fall into inauthenticity, repression of disagreement, denial of problems, into "ideology" in its negative sense as an alienating bias. Conversion is basically three-fold as intellectual, moral and religious, but the concept has led others to develop further dimensions, such as psychic, affective or political.

Intellectual conversion is a "radical clarification," and, consequently, the elimination of an exceedingly stubborn and misleading myth concerning reality, objectivity and human knowledge (238). It is a function of critical realism that liberates one more and more from "seeing what is not there" (238). Then, "Moral conversion changes the criterion of one's decisions and choices from satisfaction to values" (240). That is, one grows out of the childish condition of having to be pressured into doing the right thing, into an adulthood in which one freely chooses to do it. Thirdly: "Religious conversion is being grasped by an ultimate concern. It is the love of God flooding our hearts through the Holy Spirit given to us" (Rom.5:5). True religious conversion, far from "negating" intellectual and moral conversion, "sublates" them, or elevates them to serve the highest truth (242-243).

Other authors have developed the idea of conversion along psychic, affective and political lines. For our purpose here, however, I suggest a turn to a very specialized type of conversion theory that touches directly on the problem of syncretism, especially since it seems to propose one more version of Van der Leeuw's "transposition." I refer to Clifford Geertz's concept of "internal conversion," by means of which he examines the problem of Balinese intellectual leaders as they struggle to cope with the dominant religion of Hinduism (Geertz, 1973, 170-189). The great American anthropologist here argues that in the growth of new states, religious modernization is as important as political or economic modernization. Examining the dilemma of choosing between "a quixotic cultural antiquarianism and a barren cultural materialism," Geertz proposes to pass between the horns: he suggests that the dilemma is in all likelihood a false one, and proposes an alternative. Thus, "...the continuity of Balinese civilization can be maintained through the fundamental nature of its religious life totally transformed" (Geertz, 1973, 171).

Geertz employs Max Weber's distinction between two idealized polar types of religion, the "traditional" and the "rationalized," and applies it to the relationship between religious concepts and social forms. While traditional religion is deeply woven into established social patterns, rationalized religion sets itself either apart from or above or outside the patterns. "A rationalized religion is, to the degree that it is rationalized, self-conscious and worldly-wise" (171). Traditional religion focuses on meeting piecemeal the perennial concerns of religion—evil, suffering, frustration, bafflement and so forth. Rationalized religion is more abstract, logically coherent and more generally phrased. Rather than asking specific questions about single inexplicable events in daily life, such as why one person rather than another was killed in an accident, it asks philosophical questions. Thus, it queries, Why do the good die young? How can we know the truth? In Weber's opinion, this gave rise to the developed religions of the world and to higher philosophical systems. Aside from arguments as to the origin of religions, Geertz's interpretation of this distinction zeros in on the point of our theme: "What is important is that the process of religious rationalization seems everywhere to have been provoked by a thorough shaking of the foundations of social order" (173).

While Weber saw this as a process of "disenchantment," and so established a sharp dichotomy between the two poles, Geertz suggests that in neither the world religions nor in the local ones is there such a sharp cleavage, and that sophistication exists among all religious groups. While granting that world religions have developed their conceptualizations to a higher level, he maintains the possibility of rationalization in all societies (175). As I shall demonstrate later, my own experience has verified this argument countless times over.

Geertz turns to his own field work in Bali to develop his position. While Bali is broadly speaking a Hindu society, the indigenous religion has persisted throughout the generations of Hinduism. Traditional Balinese performance-centered religion has continued its own forms of temple worship and priesthood, sanctioned social classes and death and witchcraft cults, with a minimum of effort to interpret these practices. In other words, this is an example of "unconsciously" syncretistic popular religiosity so often described in studies emanating especially from Latin America. But Geertz's interest here lies in describing how the Balinese are addressing the challenges of modernization, and the connection of these challenges to Christianity and Islam, in order to preserve their cultural identity. This is taking place through the rationalization process called "internal conversion" (182).

Geertz does not tightly define this process, but describes it as an action producing "a self-conscious Bali-ism" that can approach the world religions in addressing general questions and finding comprehensive answers. The foremost "agents" of this conversion at the time of Geertz's study were educated or semi-educated young men between eighteen and thirty. Geertz describes, for example, a group of such youth sitting at a wake, and breaking into a discussion on how to discern the line between secular custom and the realm of the sacred. The purpose of such a discussion was to decide what elements of the funeral are truly sanctioned spiritually and which are merely accretions of habit and tradition. From this theme, a conversation ensued that involved a debate between the Marxist view of religion and the more traditional interpretation grounded in religious faith.

Such conversation as this has led further into liturgical reforms as well as to rationalization at the level of dogma and creed, resulting in a growing amount of trade in scholarly studies of Hindu and Buddhist works and even studies of the history of the local religion. More, Geertz descries in all such dialogue the origins of protest against many tyrannical abuses using the guise of religion, practiced by the secular government. Such local leaders are demanding that authority now give true reasons to justify itself rather than mere appeals to "court ceremonialism"; in Geertz's view, they are working at a development of doctrine (187). Further, such demands are calling forth a self-accounting from the old elite: a prophetic article, this, in light of happenings in Indonesia and environs in the past few years.

The many parallels with our discussions of syncretism are self-evident, and they seem to be leading in an analogous direction—from an "in-between" of intellectual and social tensions toward what, it is hoped, will be a new synthesis. Geertz thus further describes his internal conversion as the necessary "popular change of heart," explicit codification, and formally intellectualized structure that will embody these changes. It is an essentially "ecclesiastical" one, especially since there are ensuing conflicts with Catholics (who, at least in 1964, were highly separatist in relation to the government), and with the Muslims, who view all religions not of the book as an abomination. The Balinese are demanding equal recognition of their religion with the world religions of the country (187).

The intellectual give-and-take that Geertz describes between the young Balinese and the "book religions" is vividly redolent of the exchanges now occurring wherever traditional tribal religions are experiencing a "revitalization" over against dominant organized religions and secular governments. At the time of writing, Geertz professed to have no crystal ball to predict what would come of it all, and it seems that his wise agnosticism about the future was well-advised. In any case, all the more can we see in this "case study" an example, not only of the kind of syncretic tensions we have been studying, but also of the powerful role of religious, moral, intellectual and political conversion in the formulation of a critical theology of syncretism. If Lonergan had been able to examine this issue, he would certainly have expressed an ardent hope for leaders who could be attentive, intelligent, reasonable, responsible and in love with God and their fellow human beings. To carry this discussion forward, then, he would have recommended the following.

THE ROLE OF FUNCTIONAL SPECIALTIES

Lonergan's own intention for method is that it should include theology with a dynamic and progressive capacity. To accomplish this, it is essential that theologians of whatever stripe *know what* they are doing and *why* they are doing it. They must learn how to practice a theology that overcomes the "classicism" that conceives any one culture normatively and statically, hence a theology that facilitates a genuine growth within cultures, especially in the religious dimension. In order to facilitate this progression, Lonergan offers the functional specializations and an explanation of their utility. There is thus a kind of "divide and conquer" or "division of labor" approach here that comes full circle to an integration. There has to be a division and subdivision in dealing with data, and this calls for the specializations that separate out the many relevant data, classify them, and guide study along the path from data to results. That is, he recommends the functionally interdependent specialties, which he divides into eight categories.

First, there is *research*, which makes available the data relevant to theological investigation. Secondly, the specialty of *interpretation* seeks to understand the meaning of the data. *History*, in the third place, deals most basically with specific persons, places, dates, events, etc., as well as with movements and historical events, seeking a total view of all these particulars. For Lonergan, history is essential for imparting to theology the dynamic progressivism he expects it to achieve. Fourthly, the specialty of *dialectic* is meant to deal with oppositions and conflicts and contradictions—obviously a need in our context of syncretism. The fifth specialty, *foundations*, is perhaps the most easily misunderstood, since it may give the impression of permanent and unmoving classicism. However, its role is not to hammer out doctrines but rather to project "the horizon within which the meaning of doctrines can be apprehended" (131). Sixthly, there is the specialty of *doctrines*, which serves to express judgments of fact and of value, and thus becomes the tool of both dogmatic and pastoral theology. Correspondingly, the existence of doctrines leads to the seventh specialty of *systematics*, which serves to deal more in detail with questions put to doctrines. Finally, the eighth specialty, *communica-*

tions, is concerned with theology in its external relations, seeking to bring all other functions into the "minds and hearts of [men] in all cultures and classes" (133).

The first four of these specialties constitute what Lonergan calls "indirect discourse": that is, they are concerned with the theologian's own development. The second four compose the "direct discourse" vis-a-vis the problems of the world that theology must address. All of these, of course, must be interactive and interdependent, giving the theological community a sense of unified action and collaboration. And in one way or another, they all call for ongoing conversion. Without entering into the mass of detail that Lonergan uses to discuss his methodology, I shall highlight the way in which the specialties function to guide reflection on the problem of syncretism.

Research. Ironically, Lonergan calls his first specialty, research, "an enormously diversified category," and then proceeds to devote three pages to it in *Method*! But there is indeed a deep methodological value expressed here: the question is to decide which area of the method is relevant to the problem being dealt with. Thus, he writes, "My answer is to let Christian theologians begin from where they already stand. Each will consider one or more areas relevant to theological research. Let him work there. He will find that the method is designed to take care of the matter" (150). That is, if the method is "authentic," it will take serve its proper function. However, this specialty is also necessary in order to deal with diverse cultures and different states of consciousness. More important, it reveals to us how vital it is in a theology where too much uninformed rhetoric has been poured forth against the spectre of syncretism. Syncretism is "where we stand" in this book, and discovering the appropriate data in both literary and field work is mandatory. We shall see how this is carried out in practice when we develop a pastoral methodology in the final chapter.

Interpretation. Lonergan gives considerably more attention to the specialty of interpretation. Mindful of all the work done on this topic, he describes "hermeneutics" as "principles of interpretation," and connects this to "exegesis," or "the application of the principles to a given task" (153). For the systematician this means the study of literary texts, which must be read, especially if they are out of their original context, with a method that transcends "common sense." To wit, there must be a more sophisticated approach to the material than mere conventional wisdom. Thus one must develop three exegetical operations: 1) understanding the text, 2) judging how correct one's understanding of the text is, and 3) stating what one judges to be the correct understanding of the text. In turn, these operations must also be done cognizant of the "context," to which one applies "the hermeneutical circle" process that moves constantly between text and context (155). Many theologians, most notably the liberationists, have developed this hermeneutical circle in order to deal with contexts, and prominent among these is the late Juan Luis Segundo in his *The Liberation of Theology* (Segundo, 1976, 7-38).

However, within the hermeneutic circle the researcher or the exegete functions as well, and must likewise avoid reading things into the text because of biases created by his or her own context. Lonergan treads cautiously here through the mine field of "the principle of the empty head": certainly the researcher must avoid erroneous interpretations, but on the other hand cannot think that he/she has merely to read "what is there" in order to understand it through a kind of "naive intuitionism" (157). In order to transcend this false confidence, the researcher must constantly allow experience to inform attentiveness. Pursuing this point, Lonergan highlights a major problem that confronts our own theme: that is, an interpreter who falls into the stance of controversialist in order to show the absurdities of the object of study, without being aware of one's own shortcomings. Against this stands Lonergan's "self-corrective process of learning" (159).

In such a process, the interpreter learns how to progress from a preconceptual common sense understanding of one's object toward an informed understanding, by diligent examination of all the parts of the text and context. This leads to understanding of one's own common sense attitude as well as those of others. It is an understanding that is valuable, not only in the study of written texts of another time and place, but more, as leading to a deeper insight into oneself and one's motivations, to perhaps a radical change in the researcher. Lonergan calls this "the existential dimension of the problem of hermeneutics": it marks a conversion (161). The powerful discoveries and insights that may emerge here will propel the healthily self-critical scholar (following here the thought of Reinhold Niebuhr and more remotely of Karl Marx) beyond merely writing history to making history—to knowing history in the process of changing it (169).

When Lonergan then turns to the problem of judging the correctness of one's interpretation, he draws us into another major dimension of our study of syncretism, the reconstruction of the context (162-163). He asks, What precisely does the word "meaning" mean? He answers that it has two meanings: the "heuristic" meaning that guides the process of investigation, and the "actual meaning" that develops as one moves into a new horizon that becomes a significant part of one's own. Here I would add that our study must widen this dimension of interpretation: that is, what if the only "texts" the researcher has are non-literary—persons, events, objects, movements, etc? Reading these becomes an activity that is agonizingly hard to accomplish as if one were free of "context." It is one thing to critique the syncretism articulated in a written text such as those of historical books of the Old Testament, and that expressed in such a context as described by Geertz in Bali. It may well be that the "seminars" such as Lonergan recommends for theology will have to undertake pilgrimages to the site of direct dialogue. However, that dimension is the subject of the next chapter.

History. Lonergan devotes a dramatically greater amount of space to the specialty of history—significantly enough, given his passion to bring theology from classicism into an authentic historicity. Nonetheless, rather than follow Lonergan in his extended tour through historical theory, I simply select points pertinent to our concerns. Thus, his distinction between two senses of history is important: history is either that which is *written about*, or that which is *written* (175). In other words, we speak of history as actual events, and history as books and articles. For Lonergan's purposes, the issue is to disentangle as adequately as possible the actual events "as they happened" from the written narrative. This point is of immense importance here insofar as it cautions us about historical accounts by missionaries and their critics, including field workers such as ethnologists, sociologists, and the like. In such accounts we may be likely to find a bewildering narrative of distorted accounts of "syncretism" as well as unexamined prejudices against missionaries. Such texts should always be objects of a "hermeneutic of suspicion."

Lonergan calls elements into this specialty: the acts of persons and groups, their memories, their songs and stories, all other artifacts that may convey a message. One can seek for the "common meaning" that may be manifested in all these objects. One must also ask Lonergan's well-known historical question, "What was going forward?" in the groups we are studying. That is, we ask about the nature of the dynamic that generated changes in history. The historian also asks questions that may serve to help a group, as a psychologist might help an individual to overcome "amnesia" about the past, especially about how the past has affected the present.

The distinction between critical and precritical history is of importance to the researcher and to a community. In precritical history, one turns to methods artistic, ethical, explanatory, apologetic and prophetic—basically to the mythic expressions that interpret a culture. This kind of history does not qualify as the functional specialty history, which seeks, not to inspire and support the community but to interpret critically. The study of syncretism by Christian theologians must concern itself with both pre-critical and critical history. On the one hand, and most importantly, the theologian is concerned with the temporal and spiritual welfare of persons and communities, especially the "troubled" cultures described by Schreiter and Siller (see Appendix 1). The theologian, whether indigenous or expatriate, must work toward a "fusion of horizons" of his/her own tradition with the life-giving myths of the people with whom he/she is concerned. Precisely as Christians, we are concerned here with the well-being of a people, which we believe God desires. But one must likewise be aware of the "differentiations of consciousness" that have occurred and are occurring through the modern growth of reflective theology, and through interpretation in general. For example, what might a local tribal culture do with the soteriological aspects of its culture-hero mythology in relation to both its adopted Christian faith and its relations to secular society? (Starkloff, 1992)

In a subsequent chapter of his book, "History and Historians," Lonergan consumes another forty pages devoted to methodology and the art of history writing. What, in essence, does this say to us here?

Certainly, the entire epistemology of history is significant for theology as well, but our concern can be focused on Lonergan's wish to bring understanding (*Verstehen*) out of the study and interpretation of history. This can be applied, again, to the literary texts available to scholars in the quest to understand syncretistic experiences, the work of Russell on medieval German Christianity being an excellent example of this. In all, the researcher seeks to understand historical persons and events and their interconnectedness, and thus the meaning of the whole sequence. For example, in the reading of Russell's study, one experiences an insight into the enormously complex cultural accretions acquired by Christianity as it passed through the history of northern Europe.

Likewise, Lonergan treats the question of "perspectivism," which is concerned with the diverse ways in which historians may read the same text (214-220). Obviously, this is the proverbial problem of the blind men touching the elephant: only a fusing of experiences and a dialogue can lead to authentic understanding. Each researcher has his or her preconceptions, biases and skills, and, says Lonergan, we must be content to accept this in historians. But the dynamic of conversion should be at work here in order to achieve a creative development of interpretations, and finally to arrive at more informed and less biased theory and praxis. Contemporary theologians and missiologists who read accounts from the records of, for example, the Church Missionary Society in West Africa or the *Jesuit Relations* in North America will have to separate out the many inspiring accounts of courage, creativity and wisdom from a considerable welter of ethnocentric prejudices. A contemporary instance of this is the difference in the writings of mission anthropologists in their approaches to the issue of syncretism.

Dialectic. Given the testimonies of recent commentators on syncretism, such as the authors in the Gort and Siller anthologies (See Appendices I and II), that assert its quality of "contested interpenetration" of religious forms, the functional specialty of dialectic is vitally important. Dialectic, writes Lonergan, deals with conflicts, which may be overt or latent, and may lie in religious sources, traditions, church pronouncements, or theological writings. "They may regard contrary orientations of research, contrary interpretations, contrary histories, contrary styles of evaluation, contrary horizons, contrary doctrines, contrary systems, contrary policies" (235). Truly dialectical oppositions stem not merely from lack of information but from cognitional theories, ethical stances or religious outlooks, and may profoundly modify one's mentality. These are to be overcome by means of intellectual, moral and religious conversion.

Here the idea of "horizon" is crucial: horizon describes the limits and circumscription of our field of vision. When horizons are in conflict, there is sharp disagreement on what is intelligible and what is true and false, so that the divergence is always passionate. How does the specialty of dialectic mediate this conflict? Lonergan would say, especially to the missiologist, your vocation is all about "conversion," its ideal is the winning of souls to Christ. Well and good. But is this conversion ideal such a one-way affair? Are there not conversions to be reached on all sides, and certain myths to be recognized, accepted and transcended? Certainly a missionary must also undergo forms of intellectual and moral conversion in relation to the people with whom he/she engages. Perhaps one may even experience certain religious conversions, not as pulling one away from one's essential faith, but as a liberation from narrow religious perspectives in one's own Christianity. Witness, for example, the acknowledgment only recently that the Church erred in its condemnation of the Chinese Rites movement in the early eighteenth century. Centuries of dialectics were required to bring about this statement of ecclesial self-transcendence. The depth of religious conversion is manifest in such events as this. There is a growth of love that embodies intellectual and moral conversion, and thus a growth of the Church in a richer holiness.

Dialectic confronts the issue of deficiency in research, interpretation and history. That is, it is aware that history is not only a scientific process, but a moral one as well, intended to liberate the mind, deepen our sympathies, fortify our wills, and to control, not society, but ourselves. By means of dialectic, our work of interpretation in history must lead to appreciation of values and so enable us to discern what was and is going forward in history in terms of good and evil. Dialectic will then, of course, have to mediate conflicting standpoints about history, as well as opposed horizons, in hope of reaching a synthesis (245-246).

Thus, when scholars engage in research such as syncretism demands, "positions" are developed that Lonergan sees as compatible with the multiple conversions. Over against such positions there are "counterpositions," which are incompatible with conversion, and the incompatible elements must be removed. This terminology is confusing, but in order to grasp better how dialectics serves theology, we must try to clarify. To understand the idea of "counterposition" better, we must reach back to Lonergan's great study of human understanding, *Insight*. In that book, Lonergan chose to define "position" as the result of authentic and intelligent inquiry and critical reflection. It seems that a "counterposition" develops out of a reaction against what has already been responsibly established, and thus it tends in the direction of breakdown rather than development; it is an act of "naive realism," rather than a critical process (Lonergan, 1992, 413).

The work of scholarship and dialectics, therefore, is to discern the types of incompatibility, whether they are based on differing accounts of data, or on conflicting mentalities, in the hope that the parties in conflict will objectify their own horizons. Perhaps an example will help to clarify this complex idea. One scholar-missionary has discussed the famous Melanesian "cargo cults," and the mass of historical and ethnological data around them, as well as the many moral and theological judgments that they call forth (Ahrens, in Siller, 1991, 62-83). In order to establish valid positions and mediate such counterpositions as emerge as value judgments, extensive labor must yet be done both in literature and especially in the field. Theologians, again local theologians especially, must decide whether cargo cults are simply cases of group hysteria and even demonic possession, or whether they are a prophetic response to imperialism. On the surface, they might well be all of these things. We shall see other instances of similar problems in the final chapter.

Finally, Lonergan inquires into the explanation of how dialectic fulfills his definition of method as a pattern of recurrent and related operations yielding cumulative and progressive results. First, this specialty leads researchers to a deeper knowledge of the nature of the multiple conversion experiences, and to understand better whether one is stating an authentic position, or reacting with a prematurely uttered counterposition. The researcher must then learn how to recognize radically opposed statements, for example, in judgments about what really happened in history, and what "ideology" might be influencing one's judgment. In an area which deals so extensively with tribal societies, radically opposed ideologies will determine whether one decides out of a fundamentalist bias against all things "non-Christian," or out of a Rousseauvian romanticism of the "noble savage." Clearly, both kinds of judgment are grounded in bias.

Thus, a very salient point for the study of syncretism is Lonergan's remark, "Moreover, the theologian's strategy will be, not to prove his own position, not to refute counter-positions, but to exhibit diversity and to point to the evidence for its roots" (Lonergan, 1972,254). Lonergan further explains this position through some very dense comments on forms of analysis, but his point for us here is that dialectic is an appeal to theologians to grow constantly in authenticity, neither sacrificing one's sense of self nor one's attention to what is there outside the self. As mentioned earlier, I have found comfort in this baffling dialectic over syncretism by simply referring to it as a state of "theological messiness" that we must be prepared to accept as part of the complex discussion of syncretism.

Foundations. I have suggested that the specialty of foundations (the first of the four "direct discourse" specialties) may well be the most easily misunderstood of the eight. Lonergan tells us why: "The simple manner is to conceive foundations as a set of premises, or logically first propositions. The complex manner is to conceive foundations as what is first in any ordered set" (269). Without necessarily rejecting the idea of first premises (such as in "manual" or "Denzinger" theology), Lonergan understands foundations to refer to the second concept: the beginning of a well-ordered progress toward the truth. He sees here how the researcher must be open to the multiple conversions involved in exercising the various specialties. "The threefold conversion is, not a set of propositions that a theologian utters, but a fundamental and momentous change in the human reality that a theologian is" (270).

Foundation development must work within and pass to and from four realms of thought—common sense, theory, interiority and transcendence. In brief, these are to be understood as, in order, uncritical conventional thought, complex theoretical thought, thought arrived at by means of deeper self-examination, and thought arrived at by getting beyond oneself and observing the transcendental precepts. All have value: as I have explained elsewhere, using both Lonerganian and Geertzian ideas about common sense, this realm is natural to humans and is the source of spontaneity and natural discourse (Starkloff, 1994, 77-79, 284-286). For example, basic syncretism is the outgrowth of common sense mentalities within a culture, dealing spontaneously with contradictory experiences. This is a necessary and inevitable occurrence, but common sense alone leads to provincialism, ethnocentrism and "resentment" against more critical thinking that may be needed. Witness how the aforementioned demonic syncretism that was Nazism appealed first of all to the common sense of Germans humiliated by the terms of the Versailles peace treaty. To move beyond this condition, theoretical work must be engaged: by means of intellectual conversion investigators can help a community pass from more inward-turning experiences to more careful examination of other experiences.

But neither is theory itself sufficient to achieve true foundations, since it operates on the basis only of what it draws from sense experience. That is, it simply examines data. Hence, the foundational theologian must develop interiority, which bases its operations on an examination of consciousness and interrelationships among operations. To draw again upon the context of syncretism, the researcher must pass from mere theory by means of an examination of the dynamics of such practices, why they occur and how they are motivated. From this arises the need for the fourth realm, transcendence, the quality that characterizes the method followed by Lonergan as well as Karl Rahner. Transcendence in this case means, not simply a religious consciousness, but the ability to move from subjective and culturally bound experience in the direction of what is truly intelligible, true, real and good. Hence the need of moral and religious conversion, though without any specificity at this point—even for Lonergan, the profoundly Catholic theologian. To wit, the Christian theologian or missionary, while being a person of specific faith, is able to empathize with the religious experience of a "pagan" and find authenticity in it.

The foundations specialty thus seeks to develop theological categories, general and special (285-293). The general categories, operations that maintain the theologian in integrity, are too numerous and complex to detail here, but it is enough to say that they must keep the scholar truly attentive, understanding, reasonable and responsible. Special categories for assisting the establishment of foundations are religious experience, the history of salvation, and the trinitarian life as source of the life of believers. These categories deal with the roots of division and the polemical aspects of theology, and the development of a praxis that overcomes the evil and undoes the decline in both world and church. To recommend here the development of the general categories is really to recommend simply a thorough theological training for those who intend to study any field critically. To recommend the special categories is to urge an intellectual "syncretism" (e.g., as Erasmus understood it) by which Christian theologians draw both upon their own faith tradition and upon the traditions of those with whom they collaborate.

Doctrines. We have seen how the early Church and the early "fathers" (and at least one "mother"), by engaging in syncretic processes involving Christian tradition and hellenistic philosophy, developed the synthesis of doctrine that all Christians hold in common—foundations stemming from the first seven ecumenical councils. In our effort here to apply this paradigmatic activity analogously to contemporary growth in teaching and doctrinal development, we can turn to Lonergan's sixth specialty, doctrines, which, like all the others, must be carefully understood.

The historian of doctrine must turn to the primary sources, above all to the original message of scripture. Thence one turns to church doctrines, for which Lonergan takes the decree of the first Christians in Acts 15:28 as paradigmatic. From this, the progress is to the apostolic traditions such as we have seen in the earliest fathers, and on to the development of church doctrines as they arose to deal with new questions. The growth of theological doctrines occupied the later patristic theologians of the fourth century on into the period of the medieval schools. Finally, there have grown up diverse methodological problems such as Augustinian versus Aristotelian, Thomist versus Scotist, Catholic versus Protestant, Jesuit versus Dominican, Lutheran versus Evangelical, and so on. All such developments lead Lonergan to call all the more vigorously for attention to method, to knowing what we are doing, as well as why and how we are doing it. It is no mere coincidence that the negative reading of the word "syncretism" grows out of intra-Protestant disputes about doctrinal integrity, to the point that, as we have seen, the term became a theological insult. Certainly now, the whole issue has been complexified by the entry into the process of "local theologians" and charismatic leaders from local cultures.

For Lonergan, doctrine functions to communicate the concrete authority of Jesus as it has passed into his historical community; this is the normative function that, in company with the specialties of dialectic and foundations, opposes aberrations based on lack of conversion (299). However, Lonergan grasps the fact that the gospel is to be communicated to multiple cultures, and that it must be communicated in ways corresponding to those cultures. This point sets the idea of doctrine within a dynamic Lonerganian mode, a historical rather than a classical and static one, within the dynamic tension of the Metaxy. Various cultural expressions manifest the vitality of the Christian faith, something to be grasped not only by the missionary but by all Christians facing cultural change. Culture is no longer conceived statically as it was in the classicist mode, basically taking hellenistic Christianity for a norm. Thus, while *authentic* doctrine is universal, its expressions are local and varied, which means that the theologian must not hurl the derisive shout of "syncretism" whenever encountering new expressions of the faith. Such developments, which Lonergan calls "differentiations of consciousness," show how individuals and cultures pass dynamically from one stage to another in their interpretations of the faith.

Such dynamic growth Lonergan calls "the ongoing discovery of mind," again occurring in persons and in whole cultures. The development of doctrine fits into this growth, which we can equate in our context with "syncretic process" as I have defined it—the movement from syncretism into synthesis. Lonergan's sequence of development passes through the natural process of Christian synthesis, from symbolic apprehension to philosophical purification of biblical anthropomorphisms, to systematic church doctrine, and to the complexi-

ties of contemporary cultural development. Symbolic apprehension
is involved in myth, saga, legend, magic, cosmogony, apocalypse, typology. Within this apprehension there is no critical theology, since
by definition the expression is symbolic. However, even within the
symbolic world view, there is a capacity for reinterpreting the symbols, as Lonergan sees was done by Old Testament writers who employed the traditions of neighboring tribes to express Jewish symbols
in a new way, and by new Testament writers to transpose symbols
from late Judaism and hellenistic Gnosticism.

   In the early Greek councils the movement began to use systematic
meaning in church doctrine, as was the case with interpreting the
relation between Father and Son in the Trinity by the use of Greek
philosophy (e.g., "consubstantiality") in its progression to the fully
metaphysical approach of medieval scholasticism, found first in
Anselm and then in Aquinas.

   This was a movement into a higher differentiation of consciousness,
through which problems could be worked out in all areas of theology.
Thus systematic theological doctrine began to emerge, especially in
the thirteenth century. With the gradual supersession of Aristotle in
theology by modern developments in the recognition of the historical
nature of thought and of scientific method, theology moved into a
modern stage. In Roman Catholic theology at least, Vatican council
II indicated the development of greater historical mindedness. With
this in mind, Lonergan calls attention to the value of "ongoing
contexts," during which over time a doctrine might develop, in the
way that the dogma of the Trinity developed between Nicea and
Constantinople III.

   Lonergan pursues this theme of "ongoing discovery of mind" by
examining contemporary developments such as that of new scientific discourses and economic theories, and the new science of philol-
ogy in the reconstruction of thought. This increasing complexity led
to the recognition of the need for specialists to work collaboratively
to develop further methods. Lonergan has listed here the development of theology from the early Church down to controversies occurring at the time of his writing of *Method* around 1970. This includes examples such as the confrontation between the "positivism"
of Bultmann and the "fideism" of Barth. Within the present context,

we move beyond Lonergan's themes, but still guided by his method, in order to ask how a new theology of inculturation or liberation might influence doctrine in the future. These situations, both deeply affected by syncretism, require the leadership of local theologians. For example, what is to be the fate of a christology such as the one proposed by Fabien Eboussi Boulaga, who calls for a return of theology to a period prior to hellenistic hegemony? Eboussi wants to return to the historical period of Jesus himself, in order to develop a truly African theology, which must include the philosophy and world view of the Muntu (Eboussi Boulaga, 1981, Part II esp.).

The development of doctrine represents the ongoing discovery of mind through the reinterpretation of traditional materials. Thus, the nature of doctrine as a dynamic reality, leads Lonergan into the specifically Roman Catholic issue of the permanence of dogma. The details of this issue belong to a study beyond the one in which we are engaged, but it is well to point out that in a dogma (an infallible teaching), permanence is a matter of meaning and not of formula, of mystery and not of a datum. Thus, dogmas too are touched by historicity; that is, the permanence of meaning calls for an ongoing progress toward fuller understanding of dogmatic statements. This progress becomes all the more complex when it occurs in cultures foreign to the context in which the defined dogma originated. This points us already in the direction of the eighth functional specialty of communications, which we shall be examining in our final chapter.

A major issue here, of course, is pluralism, and Lonergan, ever wary of classicism, attends to the varieties of cultures as they express various differentiations of consciousness. He desires a unity of faith appropriate to being a Catholic Christian, but the unity is not grounded in "everyone subscribing to the correct formulae"—a classicism which he sees as, at best, "never more than the shabby shell of Catholicism" (327). Rather, the real root and ground of unity is the love poured into our hearts through the Holy Spirit; accepting the religious conversion realized in this faith opens one up to moral and intellectual conversion. From this multiplex conversion arises authentic Christian mission, including that to foreign cultures, where the acceptance of the faith and the truth expressed by doctrines will vary in expression. Lonergan believes that as other cultures, even though initially at a different stage of consciousness, gradually grow in understanding, they will enter into the full theological process. In the meantime, the Church, like St. Paul, becomes "all things to all people" (329).

Lonergan's exposition of doctrine opens up a profound approach to the issue of syncretism. He argues that, simply because they accept the faith, not all people or cultures may necessarily arrive at the same levels of consciousness differentiation, nor should they be either bound or forbidden to do so. This indicates a deep trust in the Holy Spirit, that God will guide the Church, universal and local. Without alluding to the problem, Lonergan sets forth an approach to syncretic process: many forms of syncretism are bound to occur as "young church" leaders in other cultures than the European struggle with the tension of orthodox faith and cultural identity. It is a challenge to the mission church that it accompany them toward whatever consciousness they may require for ongoing conversion.

With Karl Rahner, Lonergan renounces "Denzinger theology" or a "Christian positivism" of manual theology (330). Each local church must rather, under guidance (the true role of the "magisterium"), make its own progress toward appropriating the authentic truth that doctrine and dogma symbolize. Lonergan, who was never a missionary in the accepted sense of the term, expresses a profound appreciation of the role of mission theology: it must inculcate true "responsibility" in new Christians and local theologians. His words on this point deserve a fuller quotation:

> There is much to be gained by recognizing autonomy and pointing out that it implies responsibility. For responsibility leads to method, and method if effective makes police work superfluous. Church officials have the duty to protect the religion on which theologians reflect, but it is up to the theologians themselves to carry the burden of making theological choices as much a matter of consensus as any other long-standing academic discipline (332).

Systematics. What Lonergan is describing above, of course, is the work of his seventh functional specialty, systematics. This specialty has five headings, as he sees it, and these apply to the question of discernment in the syncretic process. The first heading is simply the *function* of the specialty, while the second deals with the options taken in carrying out the function. The third is involved in the question of how the human mind understands transcendent mystery, and the fourth deals with the complexities of arriving at understanding, not just "data," but truths, while the fifth option relates to the ongoing development of systematics.

First, the function of systematics is to arrive at understanding (*Verstand*) (335). Noting that Kant had equated understanding with the faculty of judgment, Lonergan (to keep our comment on this point brief) argues that there is a distinction between understanding and judgment in the thought of Augustine and Anselm. Thus, "believe in order to understand" supposes that belief itself is already a judgment, so that understanding is another dimension. Lonergan follows the basic lines of Vatican Council I here in its teaching that reason illumined by faith can arrive at fruitful understanding of the things of God, and this progress is the principle function of systematics. This renders the work of the systematician highly creative; by working facts established in doctrine into an "assimilable whole," systematics is not so much involved in establishing certitude as in promoting understanding (336). Lonergan's own example of such a process is found in the *Summa Contra Gentiles* of Thomas Aquinas, wherein the theologian discusses the existence of the persons of the Trinity, *interpreting* the doctrine in the light of the meaning of divine generation (a special problem for Muslims regarding divine sonship, we might note). This example was a classic case of how Aquinas integrated the projects of philosophy and theology. Behind this work of integrating was the need to transcend mere "proofs" and rather to transform the concrete individual so as to enable understanding of the principles behind one's conclusions. That is, systematic integration involves not only mere data-knowledge, but also conversion. Lonergan, with Thomas Aquinas and the early Cappadocian theologians, seeks to maintain the synthesis of natural and revelational theology.

Still more to our purpose is Lonergan's insistence that systematics should involve intentionality analysis, which in itself is not a metaphysical exercise but a psychological one. Theology is ultimately grounded in an act of love, the love that begins with God flooding our hearts (Rom.5:5), and is thus concerned with pure *mystery*. Nonetheless, the many human responses to this love are *not* the divine mystery, but human problems. To embrace the divine mystery does not exonerate the believing community from treating the human *problems* that arise from the primitive act of faith. To wrestle with the complex multiplicity involved here implies a constant exercise of dialectic as well as of all the functional specialties.

Lonergan sees the labor of systematics as arriving at deeper understandings of the truth in church confessions—the various instances of *Bekenntnis* (confession) that concern all the essays of the Siller symposium on syncretism. Lonergan was always aware of the dangers of elitism inherent in systematic theology, and thus saw the urgent necessity of the eighth functional specialty, communications: "Finally, systematic theology is irrelevant, if it does not provide the basis for the eighth functional specialty, communications. But to communicate one must understand what it is to communicate" (351). The enduring truth behind doctrinal and dogmatic statements demands the work of communication with each culture, which I shall attempt to describe more concretely in the final chapter on pastoral praxis.

Communications. In the function of communication, theological reflection bears fruit, and this fruit is expressed through the communication of meaning, the difficulty of which is most dramatically expressed in crossing over into a different cultural tradition. Community cannot be achieved or maintained without "common meaning," which arises only through intersubjective exchange of gesture and interpretation. For Lonergan, who is here employing Gibson Winter's excellent *Elements for a Social Ethic*, the primal foe of common meaning is the failure of conversion expressed by ideology, or "the self-justification of alienated man" (357). We need not quarrel with Lonergan's negative understanding of ideology, since, as he interprets it here, it always clouds consciousness and blocks out the openness needed for conversion. In such an understanding, ideology is indeed the basis of alienation and an insuperable block to common meaning.[2]

---

2. Clifford Geertz (1973, 193-229) and Juan Luis Segundo (1974, passim), are authors who have sought to interpret ideology from a more positive perspective and with greater nuances. But not even those understandings of it preclude the fact that ideology does inflict thought with a heavy bias.

Lonergan's concern in the area of communications was to identify the means for realizing cooperation within community in the quest for common meaning. Such community may be based on one of three principles, moral, religious or Christian, but in the action of Christian systematics, all three principles are involved. Aspects of community may be realized, then, through common meaning in a moral quest, a general religious quest shared by all religions, or in the sharing of the gift of Jesus Christ by all Christians. But none of these aspects can be realized without the appropriate conversions.

Lonergan thus concludes his study with a discussion of the contemporary situation of the Church that was prophetic at the time when he wrote it, since it antedated all the discussion of "inculturation" that grew out of Vatican II and the Thirty-Second General Congregation of the Society of Jesus. He bases his argument in this final chapter on the mandate to communicate the gospel to all nations, with the consequent obligation laid on all communicators to study the culture and the language of the people they address. We read here a succinct statement of Lonergan's rejection of the classicist and normative meaning of culture: "They must grasp the virtual resources of that culture and that language, and they must use those virtual resources creatively so that the Christian message becomes, not disruptive of the culture, not an alien patch superimposed upon it, but a line of development within the culture" (362).

Thus the Church is in process, a process of "self-constitution" analogous to what we see now occurring in worldwide human society. Since this is also a structured process, it must attend to the "good of order" in meeting Christian needs. It is an outgoing process that takes the Church into the whole of human society, and thus is redemptive from alienation and blind ideology. Within this manifold process, the Church works, not only as a theologian, but as a historian who will first ferret out instances in which ideology has been at work. It may also operate as a psychiatrist, who must identify his or her own neuroses in order to help others, or as the social scientist who recognizes alienation in his or her own work.

Our examination of Lonergan's penetrating remarks suggests the "critical theory" work of Jürgen Habermas. One of that "Frankfort School" philosopher's preoccupations is with relating knowledge to human "interests" and thus restoring knowledge from abstract aloofness back to social value (Habermas, 1971). One commentator describes Habermas's plan for such a restoration in the four steps that might serve to describe our own processes of communicative dialogue with syncretism (Pusey, 1987, 69-86). The first essential is to establish a process of reflection that all can share. The second is to facilitate intelligible speech and symbolic interaction so that the unrecognized may become communicable and public. The third is to find means to share interpretation leading to critical theory, the fourth is the consequence of the previous three—a return from distorted practices of communication back to the structures that have been distorted.

Habermas's basic model for this is psychoanalysis. He wrote in his *Knowledge and Human Interests* that he had turned to Freud for his ideas, not out of any desire directly to explore Freud's methods, but because "The same configurations that drive the individual to neurosis move society to establish institutions" (Habermas, 1971, 276). Communication can be deepened only by penetrating the walls set up by the institutions, which in themselves cater to controlling interests. In his study of the student protest movements of the 1960s and 1970s, Habermas wrote about how theories tend to become forms of technical power, and must thus be re-oriented if they are again to be dialogical and useful for creative discourse (Habermas, 1970, 55). The same must be said of ideologies: participants in true dialogue will have learned to question their own basic assumptions and commitments, and all "culturally ingrained pre-understanding" (Pusey, 1987, 84).

Especially valuable to us, then, is the insistence on the process called "speech action" by philosophers like Searle: that is, the interlacing of speech and action, of doing along with knowing (what others have called praxis). Likewise helpful is Habermas's special mention of the need for "communicative symbolic interaction," especially when conversing with traditional societies for whom myth and religion are so constitutive (Habermas, 1970, 95). If Habermas may sound a trifle condescending here, "modern" Christians do well to be aware that their own deepest myths will be involved in dialogue with those of aboriginal peoples. More important, the dialogue and tension of "contesting" myths are elements of the metaxic tension in the dialogue on syncretism.

I have dwelt here on Lonergan's dense methodological treatise because I have found it, in its daunting complexity, to indeed be "cumulative and progressive" whenever I seek to grow pastorally as well as theologically. This mention of pastoral theology now carries us into the realm more properly called "praxis"—the interaction of theory and practice, to growth in knowledge that is also growth in critical action (what Siller has called *Handlung*). We conclude this chapter in the hope that our methodology will effectively lead us through the field cases to follow.

3
INTO THE CONTEXT:
"SYNCRETIC ACTION"

We have wended our way through a history that covers both theory and practice, and through the intertwining passages of theological and anthropological method. I hope, in this final chapter, to emerge from the murkier and more tortuous pathways out into the broad plain of pastoral praxis, although this too will not lack its baffling elements. I take a cue from the various syncretism anthologies that have combined theory with examples or "cases" (see Appendices I and II). Having suggested in Chapter Two an outline for a developing theology of syncretism, I now set out by way of "field" cases to construct a fuller pastoral praxis—of theory/ action process—what Hermann Siller has called *Handeln* (Siller, 1991d, 174-184). This is fundamentally a metaphor referring to mercantile or business dealings—an excellent way to describe the manner in which theologians must "do business" with this complex partner. I have chosen examples from my own pastoral work in the field of mission among native North American peoples, where I have constantly experienced situations such as those described by some of the writers in the Siller symposium. (See Appendix I) It is my hope that these "cases studies" might help other local theologians to interpret their respective contexts.

The value of syncretic process among marginalized peoples lies in the dynamism of cultural rediscovery and revitalization. In her recent very helpful *Theories of Culture*, Kathryn Tanner highlights the significance of "life at the boundary" for creative discovery (Tanner, 1997, 115). For Christian theology, Tanner sees this discovery as being formed, not just "by" the boundary, but "at" it, through shared action with local cultures. Sketching out a very "postmodern" method for theology, she realizes the inevitability of conflict, as well as of the "contest" dimension of syncretism. In the course of this encounter she recognizes the creative labors of the cultural *bricoleurs* to whom we have referred earlier, and the need for theology to form a partnership with such as these (165-166). Sharing Tanner's desire for a dialogue rather than a monologue on syncretism, I shall be introducing readers to a number of *bricoleurs*, and will suggest ways in which to "walk with" those who may desire to serve this role as Christians within a local culture.

I propose to address syncretic process on two levels: first, I examine the surface manifestations of cultural adaptation that display a mingling or combining of symbols from aboriginal cultures with the Christian liturgy handed on to them from Europe. Thus I shall be describing the actions of Christian aboriginal persons as "commentators," who began with the aftermath of Vatican II to respond to the newly-found and at first shocking openness of missionaries, to "bring some of our culture into the church." Secondly, I attempt to probe more deeply into the phenomena of tribal practices and to understand the "intentionality" of Christians who (as we all do, in some way) live a syncretic life by maintaining a balance that contains practices from both traditional culture and the imported Church—a "dual system" or "compartmentalization," as some have described it. There is a much deeper and more complex syncretic process occurring in contexts like these. All such persons now involved in the more self-conscious tension of the search for identity and meaning in history share this place in the Metaxy, the In-Between, with our earliest Christian forebears, especially the tribal ancestors of those of us who are of northern European origin. As we progress along this "ritual process," or "pilgrimage," we must appreciate how much common ground we have with "new Christians" if we reach back far enough into our own histories.

"Bringing in Our Culture"

This phrase, employed so often by aboriginal Christians to describe liturgical adaptation, is of course a theological somersault! It is the vocation of the Church-as-mission, not to "bring cultures into the Church," but to introduce the Church into cultures. But mission history has developed otherwise, and we must deal with it as it is. The early 1970s will go down in liturgical history as a time of (among other things) awkwardness and much good-willed stumbling by missionaries seeking to manifest their openness by introducing indigenous symbolism into the liturgy, catechetics and homiletics. One example that stands out in my own memory occurred during an early meeting of the revitalized Tekakwitha Conference—the organization of Catholic Native Peoples and ministers of the Church. At the concluding eucharist, the local bishop, a man of open mind and heart, willingly agreed to carry in the procession, not his customary crozier but a "coup stick"—a symbol commonly used by warriors on the plains. They would carry this four-foot long instrument, with its shepherd's crook handle, and use it to display extraordinary courage by galloping close to an enemy, simply touching rather than killing him, and then gallop triumphantly away, having "counted coup." The similarity of symbolism in this service was that the coup stick does resemble a bishop's crozier, and that a chief would also carry a coup stick when leading pow wows. The introduction of this symbol into the liturgy was never fully explained, but no one complained on that rather euphoric occasion in the late 1970s. It was a small example of Van der Leeuw's "transposition."

However, another sign of the times took place at the opening of the Conference some two or three years later, when one local native parish was invited to lead the eucharist, with a native priest presiding. The liturgy chosen for the occasion was the "Missa de Angelis" so well known to pre-Vatican II Catholics, with all the music, though not the spoken text, in Gregorian chant Latin!

One more early Catholic ceremony to benefit from the willingness of both church and native persons to cooperate was Benediction of the Blessed Sacrament. In this rite, the traditional tribal cedar incense was substituted for the conventional imported incense normally used at Catholic services. The cedar was placed in the usual thurible and then waved toward the elevated Sacred Host in the customary triple swing of veneration, or in this case worship, though it is significant that the priest also used to receive "three swings" during a high mass. Again, the practice was well-received on the occasion, but it was still some time before elders would make bold to instruct the clergy that the basic symbolism of native incense such as cedar, sweetgrass, tobacco or sage was to portray cleansing and purification, and the cedar was administered in a large dish by means of a waving eagle feather. But the elders were willing to allow their symbol to become "multi-valent," or to express more than one meaning, even as they often do today. In any case, though, the introduction of indigenous incense into the liturgy was another case of "transposition" of a symbol until more extensive mutual catechesis taught participants the more universal aspect of cedar. It has thus now come in many places to be employed at the beginning of the eucharistic service as a sign of penitential purification, with a native leader functioning in the performance.

Another development in the liturgy was the introduction of the aboriginal drum—that ancient worldwide "shamanic" symbol—with native drummers or "singers" leading the performance. This practice of using local instruments at liturgies, of course, is not new: I can recall the use of marimbas and even fireworks in liturgies and processions on feast days in local villages in Belize long before Vatican II. However, in Belize as well, some local persons balked at this, since the marimba was often associated with drunken parties. Likewise, in outback Australia, aboriginal people came a couple of decades ago to accompany liturgy not only with their own songs, but with the long musical pipe called a digiridoo, or with clapsticks and boomerangs to keep time.

With the Amerindian drum, however, further instruction of pastors and religious educators was necessary, since the users of the drum should also attend to the types of songs, and to the reasons why each is sung. Fortunately, native drummers, to the best of my knowledge, knew which songs to sing in church and which ones belonged to another context, such as the Sun Dance. The aboriginal understanding of song adds a dimension of dynamism to worship, since music is seen as itself a form of power-communication with the spirit world.

Dance is closely related to the use of song in worship, but is a more complex issue. The various types of "pow-wow" dances, if they ever did have a directly religious ceremonial connection, are now seen as part of the sociability of the occasion. Notwithstanding this, even at a "secular" pow wow, if a dancer drops an eagle feather, a religious

ceremony is required to retrieve the feather. More clearly, the dancing form employed at sun dances is so closely bound to that most
sacred ritual as to forbid its transposition into another liturgical context. Somewhere in between these two types of dancing are proces-
sional dances in honor of the dead or of a living honoree, which
contain both secular and religious aspects. Thus, the inclusion of
native dancing at Christian worship demands extensive conversation
with native leaders. During my own pastorate in the late 1970s on
the Wind River Reservation, elders saw value in including a very
restrained "donation dance" before the cross on Good Friday, at which
the people could place small donations of money saved through ab-
stinence for the sake of a gift to the poor. In sum, dancing is an
example of how dialogue is necessary to prevent unreflective syncretism and to encourage syncretic process.

Far more controversial has been the role of the pipe in Christian
settings. Among the Arapahos, for example, no one has ever prayed
with a pipe in a Christian liturgy, because of the relation that every
pipe has with the sacred Flat Pipe. This pipe is a creation archetype
for the Arapaho people, and must be most carefully guarded by its
own related rituals carried out only by a few adept persons. In this
case, an addition of a pipe in the Christian liturgy could carry the
performers into a deeper level of central symbols and thus into a
syncretism forbidden by tribal tradition, even if the Church should
permit it. That is, the issue here would not simply be a syncretism of
"elements" transposed, but a syncretism that touches deeply on an
entire "system," to employ the terminology from the Siller symposium (Berner, 1993, 134-138).

Catholic and Episcopalian missionaries have wisely refrained, in
the years of experimentation, from any attempt to "transpose" the
pipe symbol into any liturgy among the Arapaho people. The same
must be said about the—perhaps equally—sacred symbol of the traditional "Medicine Wheel" used in the Sun Dance. In other tribes,
however, the pipe seems to be a more acceptable symbol to employ,
as do other forms of the Medicine Wheel, because associations are
not so rooted in the "power" of the total aboriginal system. It has
been used, accordingly, by Ojibways and Crees at Catholic eucharists,
and in one case a Catholic missionary has prayed publicly with a

pipe at a Lakota (Sioux) funeral, apparently with general approval but not without dissenting voices (Steinmetz, 1998, Ch.6).

We can sum up these observations about surface syncretistic practices by referring back to Droogers' definition of syncretism as "contested interpenetration" (Droogers, 1989, 20-21). There is inevitably a contest when symbols are transposed or mixed; the multivalence of symbols always means that two possible meanings arising from different cultures will be in contention. Thus, is there, first of all, a question simply of which symbols bear a meaning bridging various human experiences and therefore might quite easily be transposed? Or is it a matter of a symbol that carries such a deep local significance that it is in profound conflict with another setting and thus untranslatable? In the first instance, there is no syncretism in the conflictual sense, since in the minds of participants on all sides there is a common meaning. Such is the case with ceremonial purification, which crosses all cultures, whether by means of water sprinkling, "smudging" with incense, mind-clearing body postures, and so forth. In the second case, in which two central and fundamental symbols mingle, we witness syncretism, such as would be the case with introducing the sacred Flatpipe into a Christian eucharist. In the minds of the Christians present this might present no problem, since the pipe would represent merely another cultural element to enrich the ritual. But for traditional Arapahos, for instance, this pipe is not merely an instrument of veneration but an object of it. Those who seek unity, identity or wholeness through wrestling with the challenges presented by this conflict are the *bricoleurs*. The discussion that follows attempts to probe more deeply into this issue.

BRICOLAGE

The cases to follow come under the designation of *bricolage*, because they differ from the kind of spontaneous syncretism so common, for example in Latin America. I have already referred to that kind of syncretism (understood as "dual systems" by some) as described in the work of Monast, (1969) Carrasco (1995), and Elizondo (1997). Since I have been no more than an occasional observer of some examples of this phenomenon in Mexico City, Belize, Nicaragua and the American Southwest, I must leave the topic to others more competent. My own experience of syncretistic phenomena fall more accurately under the category of a historical process that has evolved from a dual system "truce" into a highly self-conscious exercise of transposition of symbols and meaning.

Actually, I am inclined to believe that the practitioners of a compartmentalized dual system among the Pueblos have by now entered into a similar kind of dialogue. When some eight hundred of us from the Tekakwitha Conference took part in the all-day ceremony of the Festival of St. Dominic at Santo Domingo Pueblo in 1981, this brilliant fiesta carried in itself all the elements central both to the traditional Pueblo people and to the Catholic tradition—from an elaborate episcopal mass at dawn (featuring some native singing and praying) to the full celebration of the indigenous fertility and initiation ceremonies as the day progressed. Whatever the state of dialogue at present, I believe that this event as well as those that I shall discuss all typify what I have called a certain "spatial" epistemology in aboriginal thinking. That is, native experience dwells much more within a space than along a linear time sequence, and it is thus capable of allowing apparently contradictory elements to co-exist as long as these do not war directly with each other (Starkloff, 1998, 76-80). The issue of when conflict is inevitable or not is difficult to discern outside of intimate and direct dialogical conversation.

In our search for a theological-pastoral praxis, however, I shall turn now to examples drawn from my own pastoral contexts reaching back over some three decades, some of which have continued to the present. First, rather than examine differing ritual, social or spiritual experiences, I shall reach into my memory to call into the present the great *bricoleurs* who have been so significant in my own ministerial development. It is striking and fitting that each one had his own metaphorical language to interpret what scholars would call the "syncretistic" viewpoint.

Within this array of spiritual leaders I must first salute Ben Friday, Sr., the most recently deceased of them, passing on to the Good Place during Eastertide of 1994, when I had the blessing of being there for his funeral. My most vivid memory of Ben, although I had known him since 1959, hearkens back to 1983, during preparations for the annual "Sun Dance," more properly called "Offerings Lodge." Having responded to the customary invitation extended to all the men standing around to help raise the Center Pole for the lodge, I was cooling off later with a dipper of cold water, when Ben, one of the sacred "Four Old Men," walked over to greet me and promise me blessings for taking part. As we conversed, this leader took up the image used by so many thinkers, the symbol of the "two rivers." As far as I know, this was not inspired by any literary research on Ben's part, even though he was experienced in interreligious dialogue beyond his own context. What he was referring to directly was the phenomenon of the two rivers—the Wind and the Little Wind—that flow out of the Wind River mountains from two different forks, to meander separately for some forty miles across reservation land, before uniting again to become the Wind River alone. The two religions of the aboriginal and the white people, as Ben saw it, are flowing along in this way, and will one day come together (See also Starkloff, 1995). A powerful image, this, not only because of its deep sense of the metaxic experience, but also because of its enigmatic hint of the final vision.

As I have mentioned, Ben Friday was a convert from the Episcopalian Church to the Roman Catholic Church, and used to say, with his ever-available twinkle, that he had three religions—the Catholic, the Episcopalian and the Arapaho, not only because he saw the valid elements in all of these, but because he was also a distinguished ambassador among all these historically contending factions. But this image belongs in the syncretistic categories I have described, because it calls forth so much phenomenological method and "intentionality analysis." While persons such as this do indeed participate in multiple experiences, how might the student of religions interpret their approach?

I believe that William Ernest Hocking would understand this kind of thought to be in his category of "reconception" of religions, which he believed must take place given the rapidly growing interaction of cultures all over the world. Theologically, I have always trod softly in response to Hocking's idea that out of all the religions one new reconception will emerge, but I agree that we must all hope for new and creative symbolizing in the future. Hocking too used Ben Friday's imagery: "But if the Jumna and the Ganges run together, shall the united lower stream be called Ganges or Jumna?" (Hocking, 1973, 170)

Certainly, some linguistic analysis is appropriate if not necessary in such cases as the above, for example, the question as to what "religion" would be in Ben's native tongue. Contrary to those who claim that aboriginal languages have no word for "religion," the Arapaho people have a very definite one: *bätäntawt* means "sacred actions," so that "religion" refers to ways of praying or carrying out sacred rites. Thus, this spiritual man had three special ways of praying and worshipping the Creator, though all of these could come together for him within the Apostles' Creed. It was this inclusive imagery that came home to me when I paid a call on him on one return visit to the Wind River Reservation, probably around 1990. At the end of our chat, I asked him to pray for me, especially since I was still recuperating from a severe case of thrombophlebitis in my left leg. After he had passed his medicine bag over my body while praying silently, he said simply, "Now you'll be better." Other aspects of how spirituality came together in this man's life will appear shortly.

In the second place I speak of Ralph Antelope (actually White Antelope, after his grandfather who had perished at the infamous Sand Creek massacre), whom I had also known from 1959 on and who became a special friend after I had coached one of his sons in basketball. Ralph's imagery too took varying forms, for he also was one of The Four Old Men as well as a practicing Catholic. Ralph, who often assisted us at the liturgy, as did all these elders, was the one who first instructed me on how to properly offer cedar, and commissioned me to do it, even though my policy is always to turn this function over to native persons unless I am told otherwise.

After having served for several years as mission director in the late 1970s, I was advised by several of the Arapaho women that I should request an "Indian name," as they put it to me. At this, my thought turned quickly to Ralph, and I approached him with the request. The women then went to him with several suggestions for a name, but he told them that he had prayed over it and knew what he would name me. During the ceremony some weeks later, at which three of us received names, Ralph stood behind me in the center of the floor of the old school dining hall, and placed his hands on my shoulders. He ordered me to take short steps in all four directions, and then prayed over me in Arapaho, during which I heard him to use the designation *nechi chäbisät,* or "He Walks on the Water." No, it was not Jesus to whom he likened me, but to Peter, in all his blundering good will. Ralph's prayer for me was, he told me, that in my ministering, I must never take my eyes off of Jesus, but always walk boldly toward him. Then I would never lose my faith. This old man was not only a man of prayer, but, like Ben Friday, a theologian as well, and we shall return to him.

Thirdly, John C'Hair (a name that at least two editors of articles have tried to recast, believing it to be a misprint!) was slightly younger than the other two, and had served with distinction on a transport crew flying "The Hump" (the Himalayas) during the Second World War. John was perhaps the most "cerebral" of my advisers, and could certainly under other circumstances have been by university training what he was in any case—an anthropologist, a historian or a theologian. He too was a man of many prayer forms, a "Road Man" in the Peyote Tipi, a medicine man, and always a practicing Catholic. John had what scholars now call a passion for "hermeneutics": he was almost obsessed with the desire to interpret, especially for any of the church ministers who sought his help. Thus it was John who told me of the time when, one evening at the start of a peyote meeting, he chose The Lord's Prayer. Following this prayer, he explained to all present that he used this prayer to remind them *to whom* they were praying: not to the peyote, but to the Creator who gives them this medicine.

John was also a man of the Bible, which he read regularly. One hot summer day shortly after the Sun Dance of 1983, I was sitting with him on his porch, and we talked about his recent vow offering at the Center Pole, which I figured to be not only for his family but for himself, since he had a weak heart. But one thought was on his mind, and it was about the identity of his people's Sacred Flat Pipe (so sacred that they seldom talk about it, and I myself never bring it up unless they do). He had also read the turn-of-the-century monographs by Dorsey and Kroeber about the Sun Dance and Arapaho traditions, and their reference to the Flat Pipe as the tribal "medicine." (Dorsey and Kroeber, 1903, 2) He knew that Kroeber had referred to "Arapaho fetishism" in relation to symbols in general. (Kroeber, 1907, 452) Knowing well what they meant by "fetish" (a power-filled magical object), he commented in words to this effect: "I know they call our Pipe a fetish, but that isn't what it is. Do you know what I think it is? It is *our* "Ark of the Covenant!" The power of this allusion nearly bowled me over, as the whole story of the Ark went through my mind—its truly fetish-like qualities, but more its primary function as the "place" where God took up his abode among the people. I wanted to speak to John about it again, but never got the chance. In two more days he was dead from the weak heart that had plagued him for years; sadly, because he was truly a man of the Metaxy who could lead his people through many tensions.

A fourth of these leaders was Ernest Sun Rhodes, Sr., perhaps the most closely associated of all with our mission, being a man of diplomacy and mediation with the non-native community. He was a man with a puckish sense of humor who used it to soften many disputes between natives and whites, and even within separate groups of natives and whites. He also served as catechist for the mission, and as an interpreter of symbols and ceremonies from both traditions, frequently travelling with us to conferences and church gatherings. He was one of the outstanding leaders in the revitalization of the Tekakwitha Conference during the late 1970s and early 1980s. Ernest, one of the most frequent to offer cedar at services, had a special devotion to the Sacred Directions. He always emphasized, to correct a misconception that I once voiced in offering incense, that there are only *five* directions—east, south, west, north, and the earth—and not *six* directions, as I had remarked. What I had taken for the sixth "direction" is not a mere direction, but the Creator in person, without whom there are no directions at all. Like all of these elders, Ernest did live a kind of syncretic process, but it was grounded in a *very* radical monotheism.

The fifth of these leaders was a man closer to my own age, and was to die of cancer still in his early sixties. Vincent Redman was the director of the Sun Dance, a ministry of heavy responsibility in the tribe. He possessed a calm and serenity of mystical quality, a deep devotion to his family, and a loving partnership with his wife, Florence. Like the other four, he was a dedicated Catholic who balanced his aboriginal offices with his devotion to the Church in his little town of Ethete. It was to Vincent that our mission leaders went for guidance during delicate deliberations and religio-social discussions. It was also Vincent who first welcomed mission staff members into his sweat lodge in the 1970s, when a new openness was only beginning to emerge from the years of hostility between the Church and aboriginal religious leaders.

A practical "religious action" person rather than a theoretician, Vincent nonetheless was captivated by issues that complexify the tensions of the Metaxy. For example, he it was who, at my request, conducted me through an initial fast "on the hill" (called by some a "vision quest"), and then through a second one three years later. I recall the only instructions he gave me. First, he told me to take along my bible. When I asked him, "Oh, do you use a bible on the fast?," he replied "No, but you should." Second, he warned me that "they" might come around, and that "they" might try to tempt me to abandon my purpose. "If they do," he said, "just tell them why you're there, that you made a vow and intend to keep it." Upon my asking him if I am supposed to pray to them, he responded immediately, "No! You pray only to God!" I am sure that Vincent was thinking of his native word *haw'wah'aw*, which describes the prayer given only to "the One-over-all-things"—*latria*, as we call it in the old Latin tradition—the prayer of worship.

But Vincent also had a strong syncretic curiosity, based on his desire to see a more holistic spirituality. It was voiced best one night at the beginning of a sweat in his back yard. As we sat in the pitch darkness prior to the first pouring of water onto the red-hot rocks, and thus in very intense dry heat, during his customary introductory remarks, he addressed me across the darkness. "Father Carl," he asked, "would you like to say something about how this ceremony could be used in confession?" I was hardly prepared to address this topic at this moment, feeling the intense heat and growing claustrophobia, and my "speech" was a brief one! But I have since reflected much on the point. The symbolism of purification, womb of Mother Earth, rebirth and new life on emergence would indeed be an archetypal expression of what the Sacrament of Reconciliation is about.

There were others during those years of dialogue. Scott Dewey had received his education at Carlisle College at the same time as the celebrated Jim Thorpe, and had a worldly wisdom that enabled him to approach our conversations with both humor and perceptiveness. Joe Duran was also a devout Catholic and often a daily communicant along with his wife Mary. Yet he saw no conflict with his role as a medicine man and participant in the Peyote Tipi, though he never considered himself as "belonging" to that church. Marguerite Spoonhunter, an adopted parent of mine, excelled in traditional art work and raised a family of eleven children with outstanding artistic and intellectual gifts. Agnes Ortiz, a devoted member of the Church who was always ready to perform her sacred water ceremony for special events, believed that there should be no conflict between her religious experiences. Gabriel Warren, the eldest of the elders during the 1970s who died at the age (as had to be approximated) of 96, sought to integrate his Christian faith with his love of tribal traditions, and was deputed to be the chief public praying elder at the Sun Dance. Ralph Grasshopper was a devout Episcopalian who loved to enliven our conversations with the more comical "trickster" stories of his Arapaho tradition. But I leave these memories behind to pass from a narrative about spiritual persons to a discussion of pastoral praxis, applying the tools described in the previous chapter, to the "action" of syncretic process. To place some limit on these reflections, I will examine two major ceremonial complexes, the "Sun Dance" and the "Peyote Religion," along with references to the sweat lodge, all of which are in some ways deeply touched with a syncretic tension for Christian aboriginal persons. Within these two contexts, I shall construct a provisional theological and pastoral methodology.

FIRST CONTEXT: THE SUN DANCE PEOPLE

This plains ritual, which scholars believe was developed by assembling many ancient ritual forms into one ceremony as long ago (or as recently, depending on one's viewpoint) as the seventeenth century, is not itself a syncretistic ritual—a point to be emphasized. Among the Arapho people, especially, the ceremony called Offerings Lodge embraces no Christian rituals, and its own "story" or mythology is

guarded with strict secrecy. However, I include it here because participation in the Lodge by a Christian does involve the tensions of
syncretism within the participant's own consciousness, although
Christian members have reconciled these tensions, as I have mentioned earlier.

Common to all sun dances is the fast from food and water, generally for approximately three full days and nights. This fast helps to
place the Sun Dance partly into the category of "vision quest," since
participants do pray and dance for visions and inspirations. Common too is the drum music in the form of a solemn march beat, to
which participants dance, standing in a circle around the center pole
of a lodge built of timber and shrubbery. Some versions have the
participants dance standing in one place (Arapaho, Sioux) while dancers in other tribes "charge" the center pole to communicate with it
(Shoshone, Crow). Every sun dance ceremony involves some kinds
of "doctoring" or healing ministry to persons engaged in this purga-
tive suffering. Various aspects of each distinct tribal tradition enter
into the ceremony, such as the Arapaho practice of "grandfathers" or
sponsors sharing the entire Arapaho creation story with their protegés.
The social dimension of the ceremony is powerful, since the dancers
make a vow for someone, usually a relative. It is significant here that
among Christian native persons who have spoken with me, there is
clearly a syncretic consciousness: many of them apply Christian imagery to the event, such as the analogy to the sufferings of Jesus, and
the theme of penance. In this chapter on pastoral praxis, I will attempt to describe a reflective process passing through Lonergan's functional specialties leading especially to communications. The pastoral
concern here is for persons seeking to "rationalize" (in Geertz's meaning of the term) their being part of two traditions. I also presume
here a memory of the discussion in Chapter Two.

The Sun Dance in all its forms shares with numerous rites of other
aboriginal communities around the world the characteristics of "rites
of passage," as participants undergo a separation into the liminal state,
experience a sacred *communitas*, and then pass back through a reintegration into the mainstream group, ideally converted in the sense of
a new spiritual healing or perhaps new knowledge, or both. However, the Sun Dance represents liminality or marginalization on a

more extensive socio-political level, since it serves to revitalize the native community and strengthen it in its wider marginalization within a dominant culture. That is, while not syncretistic in itself, it serves the same purpose as the various syncretisms we have discussed earlier. While the Arapahos tend to avoid political language in their version, the Sun Dance complex does serve as a ritual that builds stronger social bonds among the families involved, and especially reinforces indigenous identity in a dramatically powerful way. Among the Wind River Shoshone (Shimkin, 1953; Jorgensen, 1972), not only is identity emphasized, but the theme of cultural resistance is articulated. Thus, in the case of Christians who participate but who also desire to be part of a mainstream church as well, a dialogue with pastoral theologians should focus on Geertz's "internal conversion." Through such conversion, aboriginal persons can develop a deeper skill at reflection in order to articulate a theology of identity and independence within the wider secular world. In this process, then, the Church would encourage native persons in their practice of the native ritual as a part of their wider Christian experience, but in no way seek to direct it. Within such a conversation, the functional specialties must have a role suitable to the degree of preparation of those concerned.

The specialty of research, obviously, must be grounded in indigenous peoples' experience of participation; for non-natives who are welcomed to assist, it is based in whatever degree of "participant observation" they may be allowed to share. The native persons would to some degree, as I have described in the persons of my elder teachers, examine their experience reflectively as they seek deeper understanding, and thus take charge of their own analogous "naming"—as for example interpreting the Sacred Pipe as "our Ark of the Covenant" rather than a "fetish." They might, again, according to background and education, engage in reading literature on the subject and judging how this literature corresponds to their own experience. As John C'Hair's remarks often showed me, aboriginal persons frequently find that reading the Old Testament stimulates them to compare themselves to the Chosen People and thus indirectly to some kind of "Exodus" interpretation.

The specialty of interpretation here might focus especially on the Sun Dance as a "text" set within a larger "context" of tribal life, and on tribal life as unavoidably set within the context of a dominant culture. The "readers" of the text, whether an actual participant probing his or her memory, or an outsider seeking empathic understanding, must situate themselves between text and wider experience. There is, one might say, a deeply "ironic" use of the word "text" here, since any written text *about* the Sun Dance is not the original experience but an outside interpretation. At a deeper level, however, for Christian native persons one process of conversation would also involve a similar insertion of their Christian text, fundamentally the Bible, within the hermeneutical circle. In that case, the Sun Dance becomes the experiential horizon for the study of scripture.

The process seems frighteningly complicated, and for the more scholarly model it may be. However, there can be a very "grass roots" interpretation as well, such as the one shared by a woman whose son was going through the Sun Dance. As she beheld him passing through this arduous ceremony, wearing the customary garland of sage on his head, the suffering Jesus came to her mind, and thus a solidarity between her son and Christ.

The function of history would also be exercised in a dual fashion. First, regarding the actual "fact" of the ceremony itself, the student would seek to know all that she/he can about both the mythic origins of the ceremony as well as historical data as recorded or recounted orally by elders. In fact, some of the elders directing the ceremony have in the past consulted the monographs of Dorsey and Kroeber, especially the color sketches of the type of body paint designs used at the turn of the century. Some study of Bureau of Indian Affairs records could be valuable in the process. In the case of the Crow people of Montana, the history of their present Sun Dance is accurately dateable to 1941, when William Big Day received the Wind River Shoshone rite to replace the one his own people had lost earlier (Crummett, 1993).

On the wider canvas, of course, a second function of history would be socially valuable if native persons should choose to study all the modern history of their people, especially the excruciatingly painful history of rapine and exploitation that was American (and to some degree Canadian) frontier expansion. How has the Sun Dance served them to deal with this history? What are the "facts," and how have both natives and whites recorded or understood them? What is the history of the Church in all this? There has been a massive threefold conversion among most missionaries, both in how they view frontier history and in how they evaluate native religious practices. In sum, Lonergan's heuristic question, "What was going forward?," carries dramatic creative potential. For example, Sister Inez Hilger's monograph cites how one historian, writing in the early 1950s, that the Arapaho Sun Dance was "destined to go" before many more years would pass. What was *not* "going forward" that this writer mistakenly believed to be going forward? (Hilger, 1952, 151)

On the level of historical praxis, the role of history is vital as a recording of the narrative of elders about their people's backgrounds. Even without "scientific" corroboration of such personal narrative, without history "as it happened," these stories handed on to subsequent generations make up the essential ingredients for a liberating process, especially when the gleaning of these stories is carried out by young researchers from among their own people. Regardless of the documentary verifiability of the information, the cumulative experience of many such narratives can lead eventually to authentic "understanding" of a historical period or movement. For example, the many testimonies from native persons in many contexts of my own experience do not necessarily corroborate each others' data, but a collection of this information provides a wider sweep of history that can assist pastoral renewal. Thus, the degree to which various churches and church leaders may have attacked native traditions or tried to encourage them is generally not fully agreed upon among the narrators. What is agreed is that there is deep need for healing of relationships between the churches and native people that also involves secular government history. By comparing such narratives with mission and government archives, pastoral theologians can develop their ministry of dialogue and healing.

I have already cited a dramatic case of such careful selection on the matter of syncretism by the gathering of testimonies from elders born around the turn into the twentieth century, especially regarding primitive monotheism. This data does not and cannot "prove" a theory

like that of Wilhelm Schmidt's about primordial monotheistic beliefs, but it does produce a virtually universal consensus that in the
late nineteenth century at least the Arapaho people and many other
tribes did believe in one sovereign Creator. That this may have had
Christian influence is certainly a valid argument, but all of the elders
of my own acquaintance between 1970 and 1990 testified quite in-
sistently that their people always did believe that there was really
only "One-Above-All-Things" (*Bähätixt*), and that the missionaries
helped them to recall and emphasize this. I have heard this argument
corroborated time and again by native persons elsewhere, especially
Ojibway, Cree, Odawa and Pottowatomi persons. If the researcher is
simplistically only "after the fact," to use the clever pun of Clifford
Geertz (Geertz, 1995, 166-168), this data is of little use, but to a
pastoral theologian it is priceless.

Pastorally speaking, Lonergan's identification of dialectics with
conflict makes this specialty one of urgent importance. Given the
contextual nature of the syncretism situation and the entire metaxic
and tensive nature of the problem, dialectics must be engaged in at
all levels from grass roots conversation to scholarly research. In 1969,
for example, I offered to respond to the question of the young Arapaho
Bob Spoonhunter, "Why has the Church dealt so hard with our native religion?" I promised to research the problem and to examine
the attitudes of missionaries, little appreciating how endlessly the
dialectical nature of that question would remain with me to the present
day. In no other theological function have I or my colleagues—grass
roots or academic—witnessed such a constant weight of ongoing intellectual, moral, religious, affective and political conversion. Nowhere has there been more evidence of that to which Lonergan refers
as the issue of deficiency in research, interpretation and history.

If one takes into the dialectical mode here the whole history of
interpretation of the Sun Dance, the conflict of position and
counterposition is verified. Accepting Lonergan's definition of
counterposition as a rejection of evidence and thus as a sign of ab-
sence of conversion, this dialectic serves a heuristic function for pastoral theology. In conversation about aboriginal rituals, the modern
theologian's persistent tendency is to voice a counterposition to a
native person's statement, with the desire to prove his or her own

position, whereas what should happen is that the historian might appreciate the possible diversity of positions and viewpoints.

A classic example of this problem can be found in an error of mine committed during my earliest observance of the Sun Dance in 1970. Witnessing how the "pledger," or main vovant, followed a tractor-drawn wagon around the campgrounds prior to the opening of the Offerings Lodge, collecting donated goods, I came to a premature, and thus inauthentic, conclusion. I later described this in a book as a "begging tour" (Starkloff, 1974, 60), not meaning begging in a negative sense but in light of my own historical knowledge of the practice of pilgrims in medieval Europe. Inoffensive as my intention was, I was being not only ethnocentric, but even culturally insensitive. In theory, what the pledger was doing there did bear a certain analogy to medieval pilgrimage situations, in that he was giving people an opportunity to acquire help from the Creator, or "grace," based on their openness of heart. But when one man read this book he became quite indignant, and happily, overcoming his customary native politeness, he came to me to protest. The object of his protest was my use of the word "begging," which to him simply echoed the constant insult hurled by whites at native people: they were just "a bunch of beggars." He then explained that this was a chance for people to make gifts to the lodge "so that no one would get sick." I had lost a chance to establish a helpful analogy by my haste to "name" a phenomenon without sufficient research or consultation. Fortunately, I did not reply with an attempt at a "counterposition"! I simply apologized.

The constant temptation to give offense by establishing a counterposition in such dialectics between traditional persons and modern scholars or pastors lies not in bad will or lack of moral conversion usually, but in lack of intellectual and affective conversion. The theologian and the pastor may both be inclined to respond prematurely. The former may hasten immediately to explain his or her position before listening and reflecting, and the latter may simply be hurt and angry, or perhaps become "guilty" too quickly and do premature penance. Such events are actually opportunities to practice a learning dialectic that may clear up an error committed in research, interpretation and history. My original mistake had been in all of these specialties, and would have to be repaired by further dialogue.

As we move into the indirect discourse in dialogue on aboriginal religious experience, we must remind ourselves of the true nature of Lonergan's specialty of foundations. It is not to establish universal principles from which to deduce further principles, but rather to begin an "ordered set," or processes leading to further discovery and truth, beginning with the greater self-authentication of the scholar. In the case narrated above, I had to be called into a deeper "interiority" in order to correct what could have become an erroneous basic principle. From this movement, I had to transcend a false position and thus to develop a "change in the human reality" that I am. Thus this was the first step in an ordered set, because it introduced me, not only to new information, but to a new motivation as a practicing pastor at that time.

Not to flagellate myself too hard, I can compare my own pastoral response in this corrective process of learning to that of fundamentalist groups I have known who consider all manifestations of aboriginal ritual and spirituality to be, not merely syncretism, but "devil worship." They are thus willing even to steal sacred objects and destroy them so as to rescue souls from the grip of the demon. In Lonergan's terminology, this kind of counterposition is placed over against, not the authentic position of the other, but against the fundamentalists' *own assumption* of the position of the native people. I choose here not to try to sort out the necessary dimensions of conversions, but simply to point out that for centuries missionaries of all persuasions did establish such inauthentic foundations for mission praxis.

The specialty of doctrines provides an entry into local dialogues amid, not directly a systematic theology, but within Lonergan's "ongoing discovery of mind." For Lonergan, neither culture nor doctrine can be conceived statically, though the "fundamental truth" expressed in doctrine is an abiding one. Neither is it sufficient, in this view, to conceive Christian doctrine classically, and in so doing employ local cultural thought forms or religious understanding merely as homiletical tools to "illustrate" existing dogmatic statements. That exercise would be, not the inculturation of the gospel, but a superficial "adaptation" of doctrine to local thought forms. At a deeper level, such homiletic usages are not out of the question once dialogue partners have sought to grasp the essential truth behind a doctrine. Thus, as I have noted, the local theologian has a role analogous, though not identical, to that exercised by the early Fathers, such as the apologists and the Cappadocians. That is, local theology and pastoral care must turn to the basic source within the tradition, the scriptures, and especially the New Testament, in order to find fresh local expressions.

There is a profound historical and doctrinal principle involved in such a practice, one that third world theologians are only beginning to address. In these local situations, there is a syncretic process under way, such as that occurring among the Minjung theologians of Korea. There is a similar process going on in sub-Saharan Africa, with African scholars differing considerably on the extent to which they might liken themselves to the early church theologians. The most dramatic case in Africa, as I have mentioned, might be that proposed by Fabien Eboussi Boulaga, the Camerounian who has advocated a radical imitation, not merely of the fathers, but of the Pauline and Johannine writings themselves. In quest of authentic *Muntu* theology competent to eschew imperialistic syncretism and create its own positions, Eboussi has called for (with an exquisite irony) a rejection of the dogmatic "fetishes" that claim to control revelation, and a "return to the sources" that were in direct contact with Jesus himself (Eboussi Boulaga, 1981). This method "travels upstream" from all dogma to the Second Temple Period in which Jesus's own ministry took place, and from there to build its own properly African theology.[1] This theology then might authentically employ African thought forms, a practice that is not syncretistic in the negative sense because it is performed by local theologians. Eboussi's radicalism has not been followed by other Africans, such as Théoneste Nkeramihigo, who argues that the two-millennium era of history passing so deeply through "the west," cannot ignore or reject all European terminology and thought forms. Nor can African theology, he maintains, any longer

---

1. I am grateful to one of my students, Dr. Eugene Didier Goussikindey, S.J., now a professor in Hekima College in Nairobi, Kenya, for enlightening me on the work of Eboussi.

return to the primitive pristine purity of its aboriginal life and hope
to restore a pure African theology (Nkeramihigo, 1984).

I cite these cases, not to take sides in the debate, but because they
serve to articulate the problem of development of doctrine and they
directly involve local theologians themselves. The question of dynamic local culture meeting dynamic Christian tradition expresses
the Metaxy in its most dramatically tensive form. They illustrate the
extent to which local cultural forms might become authentic expressions of the eternal truth of the gospel. Is the basic hellenistic language of the creeds to be the only universal expression of Christian
doctrine, with local terminology serving only a catechetical and homiletical role? To what degree would a local culture change, if at all, the
recitation of the early Christian symbols of faith? The seriousness of
this discussion can be emphasized if we recall our earlier reference to
the Germanization of Christianity, during which many local practices and thought forms deeply affected liturgical practices, symbols
in general, and theological and ethical interpretation. This period,
however, did not alter the basic creedal statements at any official level,
(though we have seen highly syncretized examples of local outgrowths), but sought, in its better theologians, to interpret them.

It can be argued, as Catholic theology and mainstream Protestant
theology have, that the early councils represent a specially gifted period during which the gospel acquired a language that was then the
language of the known civilized world. in fact, when Vatican II sought
to reform liturgy and catechesis, it discarded or at least relativized
Germanic elements in favor of a return to scripture and the Fathers.
And yet, what are we to respond to Karl Rahner when he insists that
a "world Church" must truly reach out to all nations? Prudence and
not cowardice, it may be hoped, dictates that this book is not the
place to try to resolve all these issues, however much we must keep
the conversation alive. For our purposes here, I will accept the outcome of the struggles of the early patristic period to preserve the
basics of Christian truth against heresy. I thus adhere to its confession of the Incarnation, the Trinity, God's embracing of the natural
world through the sacraments, and the unity of Christian confession
and practice carried on collegially by the bishops. Christians are of
course still not in agreement about how this "communion" is to be

structured and enacted, but we can all agree on the value of ecclesial unity that respects cultural diversity, which is the issue in this book.

Returning now to the local context of the Sun Dance, let us examine ways in which ongoing syncretic processes might serve a dynamic development of an inculturated faith. Here I recall the dense reflections of Hermann Siller on two aspects of contemporary hermeneutics that serve to distinguish "good" from "bad" syncretism. The first of these is Siller's adaptation of the "communicative action" involved in the process by which a "commentator" builds a "commentary" on a "commentandum." (Siller, 1993, 181-184) His analogy casts the local (threatened) culture in the role of commentator, and the Christian text in that of object of the commentary. Obviously, a commentary is of value only if it interprets the truth to the culture so that neither suffers violence. My most memorable experience of such a reversal of commentary was a five-year process of creating, with the help of Arapaho elders, an Arapaho eucharistic text. With almost every sentence, indeed ever word, I experienced an indigenous person's "commentary" on my text.

Siller's second method of interpretation deals with the relation between "subject" and "predicate" to which I have referred. A heresy results when these two functions get reversed in theological action, such as was the case with Gnosticism. The Gnostics seem to have desired that their philosophy should assume the role of the gospel, and thus become the "subject" which makes Christian faith a mere "predicate" for its own interpretation. More concretely, the Incarnation ceased to be a historical fact as in Christian faith, and became a symbol of the "fall" element in gnostic systems. The mission of the Word into the world, instead of employing gnostic terminology after the method of Paul and John, became the mere predicate to illustrate gnostic thought about the transcendent order. Thus, a gnostic rule of faith would be, for example, not "the Christian faith is the true gnosis, but rather, "gnosis is the true faith." I shall attempt to illustrate how this model can be illustrated by some discussions and pastoral praxis among local native Christian leaders. I will restrict the conversation to those who have chosen to be Christians even while continuing traditional practices and embracing certain traditional beliefs. The actual cases that could be dealt with among Sun Dance people are manifold, but I am selecting two as examples of doctrinal discussion that might serve a creative purpose for the catholic quest for authentic theology.

The first of these cases belongs to a category that I shall call, with Eric Voegelin in mind, the anthropo-cosmological question, (Voegelin, 1958, 27 and *passim*) and the second is the central question of christology and soteriology.

Throughout Voegelin's *magnum opus, Order in History,* the distinction between anthropological and cosmological consciousness emerges at critical points. This tension has been dealt with extensively by Robert Doran in his *Theology and the Dialectics of History.* Intimately related to this tension, though not handled in any detail by any of these scholars, is the problem/mystery of dynamism and animism pervasive among aboriginal peoples and surfacing in frequent and startling manifestations among even the more "modern" of us. Mircea Eliade devoted many pages to arguing this point, but I have long believed that it receives its most valuable clarification in the great work of Van der Leeuw (1963, esp. Cc.9, 10, 14, 18), where the categories of dynamism and animism emerge constantly. These categories are interpreted especially by means of the triad of Power, Will and Form.

Most fundamentally, the object of all religious experience is Power, which defies a clear definition; Van der Leeuw prefers to use descriptions and examples. Thus, an experience of Power other than one's own ordinary capabilities makes one feel "dependent," awe-struck, fearful, "utterly other" (R. Otto), or amazed. Its most widely spread manifestation is described by the Melanesian word *mana,* a quasi-supernatural quality that the religious subject seeks to acquire in the form of "influence, fame, majesty, intelligence, authority, deity, capability and extraordinary power" (24). Power is thus a capacity that may in many ways take the form of magic, although it is in itself a morally neutral quality. Insofar as Power is the object of religious practice, that practice is a type of dynamism—"the interpretation of the universe in terms of Power, before which the religious consciousness stands in amazement," but also seeks to win over to its cause (27). This phenomenon is the first component of what Voegelin has called "cosmological consciousness," or concentration on the forces within the universe rather than on reflective self-awareness ("anthropological consciousness").

Power, however, is rarely experienced as raw impersonality, or without a personal owner, and thus Van der Leeuw proposes the category of Will, basically equating Will with personal conscious being rather than defining it in terms of the old scholastic "faculty" psychology. Will enters one's awareness by means of "animistic" experience, as one comes to realize that all self-moving beings have indwelling souls or spirits. Prescinding here from Van der Leeuw's discussion of the scholarly debate around the subject of animism (e.g. as in the famous work of E.B. Tylor), I am concerned now only with the *fact* of animism as a belief and the experience that lies at the root of all religion in some way. In sum, when Power is personified, and when it takes on a "Form" or "Gestalt," religion is animistic; to wit, animism and dynamism are found in some way in all religion, at least sub-consciously. Thus this phenomenon is not peculiar to any one stage of history or pre-history, but is an abiding "structure" in human awareness (88).

Rather than pursue Van der Leeuw any farther for examples, of which he has many, I shall return to my discussion of the Sun Dance spirituality for "cases" of this, cases that can lead to deeper theological discussion and thus to doctrinal considerations. Throughout any Sun Dance performance there is an ever-prevalent sense of Power, which the participants seek under many forms—health, visions, guidance, privileged knowledge, prosperity, liberation from or control over addiction, the healing of relationships, and moral reform. Thus the participants engage in many forms of consciousness-altering rituals, the most powerful of which are fasting and perseverance in dancing to music that is powerful and moving. Power is mediated to participants through a multiplicity of symbols—the Center Pole of the lodge, traditional symbols like a buffalo skull, a medicine bundle, and the two most sacred objects in Arapaho tradition, the Sacred Pipe and the Medicine Wheel. In some sense, therefore, this entire ceremony is "dynamistic," with power dwelling in so many realities and in the persons themselves. Insofar as the power also quickens spiritual beings, especially the souls of the persons involved, the ritual is also "animistic." But a word of caution is important here: the performers explicitly addressing, not powerful spirits, but the Creator, or "The One Over All Things," "Holy One," before whom they profess their "pitifulness" and need. If, lost in the ages of pre-history, human religion was really only magical manipulation (though I do not believe this), what contemporary aboriginal persons practice is not mere magic, but religion or worship.

Issues involving doctrinal syncretism here can be many, which mission personnel and aboriginal leaders discussed over a period of three decades. I must state first that I have never personally known an aboriginal person, Christian or not, who would deny the first article of the Nicene Creed, outside the narrower circle of intellectuals experimenting with alternate philosophies. Thus, the belief in one God, Maker of heaven and earth, is disputed as a native belief in some scholarly monographs (inconclusively to my thinking), but is universally accepted by native persons with whom I have conversed. This does not mean, however, that these persons, like all of us, are not subject to forms of idolatry—to "reversing subject and predicate" and letting the creature rule the Creator. I shall return to this point when dealing with pastoral practices.

Special syncretistic issues arise from the fundamental doctrine of monotheism for aboriginal peoples, all clustered around the response to power. First, there is the question of "fetishism," or the use of a material object containing power, for various purposes; in some cases this use of power may even bypass a fetish and simply pass through the human consciousness, although even in this case some word or utterance will be used. Thus, the doctrinal question (also an ethical one, of course) is: Regarding worship, are we ever to so admire and venerate, indeed covet, the power that is the Creator's alone, that we would seek to control it ourselves? Speaking ethically, aboriginal societies find themselves addressing the two related problems of sorcery and witchcraft, both of which still flourish today in some areas. Sorcery is deliberately "making medicine" against others, the manipulation of sacred symbols against another person or family or community. Witchcraft, which is very common especially in sub-Saharan Africa today, is an English word used to denote a more subtle kind of activity that seems to happen especially in socially troubled cultures.

It too harms another, but may occur through the agency even of a person who is innocent of willing it.

I have had the opportunity to discuss witchcraft with many Africans and especially in the context of pastoral ministry, such as within a mission planning seminar in Enugu, Nigeria in 1996, where it was believed necessary to include this topic among urgent issues to be addressed, along with the terrible problems of famine, war and genocide. More frequently in the past, I was called on to deal with "bad medicine," or sorcery, by means of crisis-counselling, pastoral preaching and adult education sessions. I shall enter into some detail on this below.

All the foregoing touches upon soteriology and christology, of course, since for the Christian all grace is God's self-communication in Christ, and all spiritual power is mediated through him. But further issues emerge in relation to Jesus Christ among aboriginal peoples. Local theologians must address the irreducible mystery of the divinity of Christ: since they are, and as many claim, always have been "radical monotheists," they are inclined to ask how Jesus Christ can be equal to the Father, and how the Holy Spirit too is another equal person. As my old adviser and teacher, Ralph Antelope, once expostulated in the midst of a lively group discussion on the Trinity, "Let's not forget who the Big Boss is here!" This is a question to the universal Church, whose missionaries have always sought to steer "pagans" away from idolatry and "false gods" to worship of the One God.

The doctrinal issues behind Christ as the one source of grace, and of the unmerited grace of Christ, also touch deeply upon indigenous spirituality, even if we prescind from those instances in Latin America where Christ is seen simply as one of the "Santos." Let us look at another example. In the course of an evening of spiritual sharing among our pastoral staff during the mid 1970s, we were discussing our personal experiences of Jesus. A young woman on the staff, herself perhaps coming to grips with several profound issues in her own life, spoke fervently of the freedom she felt in realizing that her justification comes, not from her own merits but from God through Christ. The response of our native catechist to this reflected his own history. Did she mean to tell him that God thinks nothing of all the years during which he hitched up his horse to a wagon in sub-zero weather in order to come to church early on Sunday morning? This protest, certainly, could be heard to come from many Christians, especially Catholics, but it is one especially proper to native persons, for whom spiritual power is not simply "given," but is also "made" through their own devoted actions. For example, the Sun Dance, along with the central rituals of all tribes, are annual "remakings" of the people. Certainly, many theological distinctions can be made here, especially between justification and sanctification, but in future syncretic processes on the local level, native leaders must have their input into the "development of doctrine." That is, they must have the role of "commentators" on Christian "texts."

The function of systematics offers both more intensive challenges and more helpful encouragement to local theologians dealing with syncretic issues. We recall that through systematics Lonergan would have us approach the gift of "understanding" as a *judgment* based on the earlier judgment of faith. Thus we are seeking not "certitude" so much as deeper insight by means of interpretation, which such greats as the Cappadocians, Anselm and Aquinas developed by means of a synthesis of philosophy and the truths of the gospel. In this process, philosophy was not an "equal partner" to the gospel but rather its servant, which they employed in order to arrive at a deeper and more enlightened confession of faith. And not only are we discussing confession here ("creed") but "code" as well: the issue, especially among the marginalized who are so drawn to syncretism, is how to *ground* doctrine and not just store it away in formulae.

This brings us back to the delicate matter of how "reason" (human mental processes more widely understood) is to figure in the development of doctrine beyond the hellenistic language through which it was "universalized" in the European world of Rahner's "second epoch." Can the use of indigenous thought forms from other cultures truly enter into systematic theology and not simply into pastoral communication and homiletics, important as they may be? I cite one example here that I have addressed previously (Starkloff, 1992, 1995). Following the lead of many scholars in anthropology, I came to realize that my quarter century of interest in "culture heroes" and/or "tricksters" was more than a research curiosity. The culture-hero, whether identified with the trickster or not, was a soteriological fig-

ure to native peoples. That is, he (or sometimes she) was the origina-
tor of all the gifts that enable a people to survive and prosper on this
earth. Not only that, this being is sometimes even the creator of the
physical world, and of all living beings. In Arapaho tradition, the
spirit-being called Whirlwind Woman, after the culture hero had laid
out the earth from primeval mud, flew rapidly around the new creation to expand it to its present size. There is even some evidence
that the name of the culture hero came to be identified with the
person of Jesus among Christian Arapahos.

Since modern native people usually do not concern themselves with
these stories as "historical fact" but as symbols of their origin and
destiny, there does not seem to be a problem of doctrinal syncretism
here. However, if Christian soteriology is to be enriched by local cultures and further interpreted through their symbolic language, as
Greek culture did for early Christians, what is the function of systematics in this? Can the theologian develop a theory of inspiration
or revelation that will involve local symbolism and teachings? So if
the culture hero looks to the temporal well-being of his or her people,
they will ask, what is this being's relation to the role of the Christ
among the people today? How would the New Testament theologian
further develop a theology—actually a social ethic—about the earthly
ministry of Jesus in light of this? Among the Ojibway people, their
main culture hero, Nanabush, unlike his more foolish counterpart
Nihawtha among the Arapahos, is emphatically separated from the
evil side of the trickster character, and becomes very much a savior
figure whose most important role is to elevate the people by teaching
them through example, even of his own "mistakes." At what level of
systematic development does one place these stories so that they might
enrich the Christian tradition?

One of the most moving and disturbing contemporary portrayals
of Christ the Crucified is the by now quite famous "Tree of Life"
painting by Ojibway artist Blake Debossige, now housed in the main
chapel at Anishinabe Spiritual Centre in northern Ontario. This is
certainly a syncretistic creation, depicting the corpus fastened to a
tree of many branches. The body itself is androgynous, thus resur-
recting the ancient symbol of totality in the human personality. The
tree, the evergreen so expressive of everlasting life among native peoples

and others, is host to a startling array of figures—birds to depict
souls of the ancestors, other animal and semi-human forms and faces
to depict other spirits. Arising out of the ground to devour the butterflies that hover around the base of the tree are subterranean ser-
pents, but the butterflies are ever out of their reach around this tree
of life. All around the painting are several concentric circles that symbolize perfection to the Ojibways. The question here for the
systematician is: How does this form of teaching affect the overall
development of Christian eschatology to render it less foreign to native peoples whose world views differ from those of western Christianity? The fact that the Sun Dance center-pole is also often described as "tree of life" draws that ceremony into the dialogue around
systematic theology.

Lonergan makes "common meaning" central to the functional specialty of communications—common meaning within a culture and
common meaning between cultures. In a brief space in his *Method*
he develops a sketch of a fundamental missiology relating the Christian faith to local cultures. His insistence that Christianity must not
be merely a disruptive message, "an alien patch" on an old garment
(Lonergan, 1972, 362), but rather a line of development within the
culture, antedates later theories of inculturation. The enemy of common meaning is ideology (in Lonergan's interpretation always a means
of self-justification for the alienated person). I shall briefly indicate
here some pastoral and social implications based on the Church's
relationship to local culture, specifically in this case the Sun Dance
theme, as we seek to develop a process of "syncretistic commerce" or
active interchange (Siller's *Handlung* terminology).

The history of genuine communication between aboriginal traditions and the Church, with few exceptions, is very brief, reaching
back little more than a quarter century. This process has thus scarcely
begun and can be further developed only insofar as native persons
are deeply involved in it. However, "communicative action" begins
with a gesture of openness, such as when Catholic missionaries, taking a cue from Vatican II, began to establish contact with native spiritual leaders hitherto seen as anathema, not simply to influence them
but to learn from them. The early stages of this interaction were
fraught with tensions, based largely on surprise amounting to shock

among the aboriginal people, who had come to expect only rejection of their sacred traditions. At times there was even dismay among those who had renounced their traditions and become "conservative" Catholics. They had come to prefer the Latin Mass, rosaries, novenas, relics, and the like (which, as a matter of fact, bear many common traits with aboriginal usage of spiritual objects). Some of these persons, of course, embraced all of these along with their traditions in the grand spontaneous syncretistic sweep that I have described. What missionaries had to do in all this was to look and listen, to practice what I have described as the phenomenological *epoché* along with intentionality analysis. Thus entered into the drama all the specialties of research, interpretation, history and dialectics, so well practiced on the grass roots level by William Stolzmann during the 1970s, with his regular dinner conversations among Lakota medicine men and local Christian clergy (See Stolzmann, 1986).

Missionaries were coming to realize that a particular spirituality belonged to this process. Part of it would be "participant observation" for the missionaries, whenever, and to whatever degree, they might be allowed to share in native rituals. Within this practice, they might "pass over" into the native experience, to use a phrase made famous by John S. Dunne to describe the entry into the ways of another religion and culture (Dunne, 1972, 154 and *passim*). This practice was far less demanding, as it turned out, than the more painful experience of "hearing" all the stored-up anger and sadness of countless native persons, and being denounced at the very moment when we were, as we thought, trying to be "the good guys"! However, not only did the exchanges afford occasions for openness and humility, they also opened up the specialty of dialectics.

Given a period of such tension-filled engagements, however, missionaries were also enabled to participate at a deeper level of communication than ever before. Not only did they become privy to a deeper understanding of the catastrophic social "strain" suffered by native people, but they became better equipped to accompany them through spiritual and social struggles. One vivid memory that I have of this kind of social communication involved the aforementioned problem of sorcery. Prior to the learning process, I suspect that my own response (or reaction) to any incident of "bad medicine" would have taken one or two forms. In the more zealous days of the missionary Church's polemic against tribal traditions, had someone come to me to tell me that he or she had been cursed, I would no doubt have admonished them that this was an inevitable outcome of their having dabbled in such superstitious practices. Or, in a somewhat more benign and compassionate tone, I might have told the person that his or her problem was purely imaginary, since such powers do not really exist. Later there was also a brief, more romantic period, when I would perhaps have told the person that this was a misunderstanding of tribal religion, which does not practice such awful things. None of these is good pastoral communication.

What we did learn to do, however, when confronted by the reality of sorcery and its effects, which often led to disasters like homicides, car crashes and "accidental" deaths, was to call onto the scene persons who were adept at interpreting for us. We learned that the practice of such rituals perhaps sometimes had served as a kind of social control, a form of aboriginal "law and order." But more, we learned that tribal spiritual leaders viewed sorcery as an abuse of religious power and symbols. Many native interpreters in North America used an image that might be expressed as "What goes around comes around." That is, one who sends out hostile power sooner or later experiences it returning to him or her, thus reversing their own power against them.

Having to deal with the problem in several cases, I developed the practice, not of denying the presence of the mana-power under question, but rather of arguing that all power, like all creation, is given by the Creator for doing good. Authentic practice of religion will receive power from God for healthy social and spiritual purposes. On one occasion I turned to christology, and preached that good power resides perfectly in Jesus Christ, and that his power is more than a match for evil use of power. We must simply trust in Jesus, pray and worship, be just to others, and try to live a good life. To one who sincerely tries to live in this way and to trust God, no evil use of power can do harm—a simple formula certainly, but acquired only through painful learning. Not long after this, I heard Father John Hascall, A Capuchin priest and an Ojibway, employ the "comes around" argument in a creative way. Yes, he argued, power does go in a circle, but if it is sent in our direction in an evil attitude, we can send it back in a good and healing way through prayer and forgiveness. Again, this is a syncretic prayer and worship process that approaches a synthesis not unlike that achieved by the great fathers and scholastics, but at a grass roots level.

SECOND CONTEXT:

THE PEYOTE MOVEMENT AND NATIVE AMERICAN CHURCH

There remains a briefer case study that can serve others in dealing with latter-day religious "revitalization" movements that may have arisen in their contexts. In this exercise I shall treat that aboriginal but highly adapted religious practice that more explicitly displays a syncretistic nature than does the Sun Dance, even if the consciousness of many of its participants may be syncretistic. I refer to the plains tradition of the Peyote Religion, in the context of which I shall again employ the functional specialties.

In the peyote tradition that has developed north of the Rio Grande since the turn of the twentieth century, we witness a sort of syncretism even apart from Christian elements. Peyote is indigenous to Mexico, and has been used ritually for centuries, perhaps millennia, especially by the Huichol people (Meyerhoff, 1974). But it was discovered around 1900 by several aboriginal persons from north of the border and developed into a distinctive ceremonial complex peculiar to the plains tribes (see Aberle, 1982; Labarre, 1970; Lanternari, 1963; Slotkin, 1956). The developed rite is thus syncretistic both within the native context, and in its relation to Christianity. This point will be significant for theological and pastoral analysis.

The use of peyote as a sacramental substance or a sacred "medicine" in the wider sense understood by aboriginal peoples, can be traced back, as I have observed, to prehistoric practice in Mexico. Sometime around 1900, however, several northern tribal searchers, the best known among them being the Winnebago John Rave, the Caddo-Delaware John Wilson, and the Comanche Quanah Parker, traveled to the border area, where they experienced visions or dreams of Peyote calling or singing to them. They harvested some of the "buttons" (or flowers) from the *peyotl* cactus called *lophophora williamsii* by modern scientists (Labarre, 1970, 10-22). This period was, be it noted, directly on the heels of the tragic demise of the protest Ghost Dance movement at Wounded Knee in 1890; thus native peoples were seeking desperately for some means of personal and cultural survival. Out of these discoveries has grown a version of North American peyote ritual usually called "peyote meetings." In 1918, peyotists, in order to defend themselves against attacks by the United States government, sometimes abetted by missionaries, incorporated themselves as The Native American Church, thus obtaining the protection of the First Amendment. This protection has held for native peoples everywhere except in Oregon, where ritual use of peyote is still illegal. As Labarre has observed (8 and *passim*), some highly Christianized versions have developed over the years. It is not my purpose to enter here into the wide scholarship on this subject, which Labarre has covered so well, but to devote my attention to the peyote phenomenon as a case of syncretism. Thus, it will be helpful at this point to return to a distinction in the study of syncretism, as elaborated by Ulrich Berner (Berner, 1993) Berner examines syncretism on two levels, the system level and the element level, allowing for some merging of the two levels in certain cases.

System syncretism (a rare occurrence, says Berner) occurs with the breaking-down of boundaries to allow a free combination of heterogenous elements in one unified religion at the cost of the identity of another one. This type occurs, for example, in African theologian Charles Nyamiti's identification of the God of African tradition with the God of Christianity by means of a "fulfilment theory" that "deepens" the African idea of God and thus obliterates the boundary of theodicy. This position is in contradistinction to the position of the Kenyan Protestant S.G. Kibicho, who also identifies the two ideas of God but insists on maintaining a pluralism. In Nyamiti's viewpoint, the African system has been transcended and fulfilled in Christianity. In sum, system syncretism changes the nature of a whole cultural complex or absorbs it into another complex.

The element level has been employed by some African theologians who seek simply to utilize African concepts to develop a new Christology. Nyamiti appears here as well by using the concept of ancestor to develop a local understanding of Christ as one example of the "point of contact" between African religion and Christianity. This too is based on the fulfilment theory, in which an authentic Christian tradition is enriched by other elements but not altered in its basic identity. The tribal religion in itself is not altered but simply lends some of its ideas or concepts to Christianity. I add here my own observation that, if one is dealing with inculturation of the Christian gospel and thus the embracing by a culture of essential Christianity, we then have a "fulfillment" kind of syncretic process. What has happened in the peyote tradition is that this system has absorbed certain Christian symbols and ideas, thus employing an "element" syncretism for its own purposes. However, the complexity is compounded here, since many Christians belonging to mainstream churches pray at peyote meetings even though they do not consider themselves to be members of the actual Native American Church. In this case, peyote prayer practices become simply *elements* within the person's Christian life. I shall attempt to iron out this convoluted phenomenon.

To begin with, the peyote ritual, as it has developed, is certainly a system syncretism: that is, it has adopted the central medicine of the Mexican tribes into a distinctively different ritual and world view, based on the common ecstatic experience obtained through the ingesting of peyote. The condition is brought on by peyote, taken in various forms—chewing the dried buttons or the buttons ground up into a powder, by drinking a form of peyote tea, and sometimes by mixing some of the powder into the large corn-shock cigarettes used in the rite. This condition, as far as I have experienced it or as far as native persons have described it to me, is not a violent one, although Carlos Castaneda has described more convulsive reactions in some who took large quantities of the medicine (Castaneda, 1977, 74). The more moderate quantities of peyote taken in meetings I have attended, after some initial nausea, does produce an altered consciousness in the form of bright colors, of beautiful expressions on the faces of others, a highly benevolent attitude toward all, and sometimes visions not unlike those obtained on a "vision quest" fast. Some also experience feelings of sadness, but these seem usually to result in a kind of confession of sins.

Peyote ceremonies vary as to location, such as a house, a tipi, or a special hut, but on the plains the common shelter is the famous tipi. Meetings, or services, begin at sunset, when participants line up behind the "Road Man" (or guide along the "way") and other leaders at the entrance of the tipi. After blasts on the eagle bone whistle, all follow the Road Man into the lodge, walking to the left and clockwise around the interior of the tipi until all have arrived at their place in the circle. There is then a speech by the one "putting up" the meeting, stating his desires and intentions, and welcoming guests. An opening song is begun on the peyote drum—a heavy metal pot on small legs, containing blessed water and several small stones, with a rawhide membrane spread tightly over the top and lashed in place with rawhide thong. The hypnotic beat of the drum imitates a rapid human heartbeat, and it is accompanied by rattles, whistles and songs. This drum passes around the tipi during the night to those who wish to play and sing, with the singer holding a special staff decorated at the top with eagle feathers.

There is a large fire near the center of the tipi, that has been lit even before the entry rite, and this is tended all night long by the "fireman," who banks the coals into a brilliant red half-moon heap. I have heard also of a "crossfire" design used in some ceremonies. After an opening ceremonial smoke of rolled paper cigarettes, the peyote is passed around in both solid and liquid "tea" form. The singing continues throughout the entire night, but because of the temporary nausea induced by peyote, a break is called sometime after midnight to allow those who feel the need to go outside to vomit. After resumption of the singing, there is a constant mingling of songs, personal testimonies, confession of sins, "doctoring" for those who call for it, as well as speeches of admonition to young persons who are present. At sunrise, the music ends, and special speeches and testimonies are welcomed. The woman of the house sponsoring the meeting enters the tipi, sits near the door, shares a brief smoke, and gives a speech thanking all who came and speaking of the needs for which this meeting has been called. This is accompanied by a symbolic breakfast consisting of meat, corn, fruit and water. Later, when the symbolic meal is finished and speeches have all been completed, at least in good weather, participants may have a larger breakfast, lie about for a large part of the day and relax in camaraderie.

I have noted that, related to ancient Mexican usages, the peyote religion is what Berner calls a "systematic" level of syncretism in that it absorbs an ancient symbol into a new system, but it is also an element syncretism in that is employs elements from Christianity. This relationship to Christianity varies widely, and presents a daunting challenge to classification. For many participants, the Native American Church *is* the Church, and they attend no other, however many Christian elements they may include—the Lord's Prayer, bibles, crosses and medals, scripture references and rosaries, for example. This ensemble defies even Berner's ingenious classification, since there is such a wide diversity of members at so many meetings. In my own pastoral experiences, I have found myself relating to many persons as practicing Christians who also pray in "the peyote way," as well as to Native American Church communicants with whom I carry on a "wider ecumenical" relationship as a dialogue. Nowhere have I seen greater need for a dialectical sense of pastoral theology, or even an acceptance of the provisional "theological messiness" that I have referred to earlier.

For other participants, those for whom we must have special concern in this book, their loyalties are to one of the mainstream churches. Thus, on the Wind River Reservation, I knew persons who carefully scheduled their meetings for a Friday evening rather than a Saturday, lest they miss church on Saturday evening or on Sunday morning. The theology of the peyote prayer is in itself quite simple—belief in the one Creator-God who gives life and all good gifts, grants visions and healings, and who might also punish. There may be entreaties to various spirits, although this was not the obvious intention in meetings I have witnessed. The ethic is also simple on the individual level: be respectful to others, be faithful to your spouse, be sober, be honest and prayerful, do not be violent—in general, elements of the Decalogue. The social ethic is not so explicit, but it is clearly an ethic of cultural survival and social healing, as well as of peaceful resistance to the dominant society. During meetings I have shared, one would hear prayers offered to "*Ho Bätän*," or Holy God. Again, the entire ceremony is one of great complexity as far as clear identity is con-

cerned, since one cannot determine whether or not the theology here
is re-creating Christian concepts into a new system, simply using
elements with a new shading, or, as in the case of many I have known,
simply doing what they do in Church, but within this distinctively
cultural form. In sum, all these traits afford the peyote prayer, arising
at it did out of late nineteenth century chaos, a very distinctive symbolic (and very syncretic) role in the Metaxy of the human search for
meaning. Beyond all doubt, it stands for many as a center of identity
within an experience of marginalization and oppression.

Theological Analysis

Much of the analysis applied to Sun Dance experience holds in the
case of peyote ritual. But since this latter is more openly syncretistic
than is the Sun Dance, a brief special analysis is called for. To begin
with, the metaxic element is powerful in this religious experience,
since it is a peaceful replacement of the Ghost Dance. In that ritual,
though it became militant only with the later Sioux peoples, native
peoples did have the hope that if they all practiced it faithfully by
performing the dance and giving up all things brought by the white
people, the whites would disappear or perhaps go back where they
came from. The peyote religion looks rather to peaceful co-existence,
but seeks to preserve a true Amerindian identity in the face of cultural destruction. Thus it is not only a symbol of the In-Between, but
also an example of Turner's liminality, which he believes is a means of
reforming and revitalizing society and culture. It is a symbol of the
space between the dying old world and a new and hopefully re-cre-
ated new world. Indeed, it is also a classic case of *bricolage*, in which
religious leaders seek to build new saving features into a culture.

Peyote rituals, by whomsoever practiced, can be understood in the
light of Turner's dramatic ritual process. While any ritual is in some
sense a "passage," or rite of withdrawal, separation and reintegration,
the entire peyote complex is a liminal process on the temporal and
spatial scale, providing a *communitas* for all its members to enable
them to live on the margins of the dominant world of the white
people but with their own cultural identity. Thus, in one sense, these
people choose a separate religious identity and a liminal position to

sustain them within the one socially imposed upon them. All in all, the peyote phenomenon fits dramatically into the entire discussion of the Siller symposium, serves as a classic example of syncretism as a process of the Metaxy, and manifests itself as a "religion of the oppressed," in Lanternari's terms.

How then is our previously delineated theological method to respond to this complex reality? Again, the functional specialties serve as an effective means to develop a theology of the In-Between. First, a phenomenological *epoché* is a mandatory response to this challenge: one who would *understand* it must practice a disciplined "bracketing," not of one's faith, but of premature judgments, and must also enter into the "intense focus" that the word *epoché* connotes, and probably of "participant observation." It would be utterly impossible for me to write even this short analysis had I not been invited into meetings by the kindly Frank Tyler family and carefully coached by John C'Hair. This entire experience, then, was both "research" and "history" carried out at the grass roots.

The function of interpretation seeks out categories that will lead to "understanding" at the level of experience, the goal of all hermeneutics, and thus will call forth at least further intellectual conversion. In the context of pastoral theology, the interpreter has as "text" the entire peyote complex itself, which needs to be understood in all its parts. Thus one will read extensively in literature available on the subject, even while trying to understand the movement of the action itself. Hence, conversion is necessary, in the form of the different conversions undergone by the first-hand researcher (the native persons themselves), and the second-hand researchers, such as pastors, church ministers, and scholars. Intellectual conversion takes place as one understands the "horizon," or all that makes this movement real and vital to its members. This must include the past century of tragic history and the history of Christianity which so influences them now even if they do not practice active church membership.

Moral conversion occurs as the student of the movement embraces a more expansive and other-directed set of values, striving to transcend mere self-justification and to embrace what is good in this movement. Thus too, the native student of this tradition will reassert commitment to the reformed life demanded by the peyote prayer, as well as a deeper interest in the common good, both of the tribe and of the human community. All who are involved in this conversation must seek to interpret and embrace whatever universal values can be shared. Religious conversion, then, for the Christian, is not a change of allegiance, but an embracing of a deeper love of God and neighbor that can be discovered in the authentic values espoused by the peyote tradition. Therefore, too, the affective conversion is not the mere "high" brought on by peyote, but the removal of psychological blockage to other conversions. Any service to the community that results from this constitutes what some have called political conversion.

The specialty of history needs no further extensive elaboration: what is important is that a researcher grasps both the precritical and critical history of the movement as a means to understanding. Precritical history will reveal the basic mythology or "story" of the origins of the movement, as well as experiences gained from the narrative of contemporary members, which usually features their complete life stories. Critical history will focus upon the recorded origins of the movement, but will also study the history of the political and military struggles that so devastated the aboriginal tribes of this continent. Obviously, as Lonergan notes, a careful appreciation of "perspectives" is urgently required.

The key to the specialty of dialectic here is to understand the nature and causes of the conflict that has permeated the story of this movement. The horizons that limit all our respective visions have to be examined and transcended if dialectic is to be creative. If syncretism, as we have seen, is "contested religious interpenetration," the researcher must examine the contesting elements, the positions and counterpositions in Lonergan's use of these terms. Both positions and counterpositions may occur in native persons and non-native interpreters. A native person may establish an authentic position that peyotists worship one God and not idols or magical potions, and the non-native person may transcend a previous counterposition that accused all native spirituality of being "superstition."

On the other hand, the non-native theologian/pastor may set forth a position that Jesus is not just the white people's "culture hero," much less their "medicine" by which to destroy their enemies, as

Jesus was perceived quite understandably by some natives (Storm, 1972,192-193). It may be with great emotional difficulty that the aboriginal person will be able to put aside his or her negative counterposition about the Church's Jesus Christ. Such conversions in all parties to the conversation in itself promises an authentic shared metaxic responsibility toward further order in history.

The movement toward a more authentic foundational specialty also involves distinguishing among and dealing with the realms of common sense, theory , interiority and transcendence, all of which are active in all researchers in some way. The common sense of the peyotist shows itself in his or her "practical wisdom," such as expressed in the contemporary proverb "Peyote and alcohol don't mix." This saying definitely has truth in it as a moral exhortation to move one to a converted decision for sobriety. For some, however, it may be simply a sort of magic formula that should work *ex opere operato* [2] and will thus constantly disappoint, because the syncretic process has not been accompanied by a transformation of consciousness. Thus, the peyotist may have to supplement his or her viewpoint by a deep engagement in psychological and theological reflection, as well as by a closer relationship with the "Higher Power" of the Alcoholics Anonymous movement.

Non-native theologians may still retain certain uncritical common sense assumptions about all native spirituality as witchcraft, idolatry, even "devil worship," and about the peyote movement itself as a mere excuse for "getting high." Thus, they must turn to a deeper study of history as well as to the testimony of native witnesses in order to develop a sounder theory. The interiority of the Christian researcher must then lead in the direction of the various conversions described above. In fine, the specialty of foundations enters into this process as not only the "ordered set" of insights and positions but as the deepening authenticity of the theologians themselves.

The specialty of doctrines is a fruitful process of creative discovery in the study of syncretism. The peyote tradition, because of the influence of Christianity (even to the point of the "christianizing" of some meetings), is ripe for dialogue with the mainstream churches

---

2. A technical canonical phrase, translated roughly as "by the work accomplished," that sees a symbol achieving results apart from the intentionality of the practitioners.

about doctrine. The movement is a concrete example of a local tradition that becomes a "commentator" on the Christian traditional "text," in Siller's use of this "communicative action" image. This does not mean that the commentary necessarily articulates a fully orthodox Christian viewpoint, but that the action does enable a local and "perplexed" (*betroffen*) culture to share in the function of historical subject rather than serving as a mere object for the foreigner's speculation. In one further way, then, this movement serves as a "passage" for Christians who do choose to be active members of a mainstream Christian church, and thus as part of the drama that renders them stronger church members.

I have cited earlier the example of Arapaho elder Ben Friday, Sr. As a local "commentator," Ben could present many challenges to the mission Church. I have beheld him at wake services (which are generally in themselves a syncretic combination of native and Christian symbols), approaching the casket of the departed and addressing the deceased in a loud voice. "You are gone now to a better place, but here we are, still poor and needy, in this world. You can still help us and pray for us. Have pity on us." This in itself is a commentary on the doctrine of the Resurrection, containing in itself traces of both aboriginal notions of life beyond the grave and the orthodox teaching of the New Creation. Here is a powerful pastoral "point of contact" between Christian tradition and native tradition, understanding the term, not, as Karl Barth always rightly objected, as being some meritorious possession of a human power, but as a gift of God that is a "seed of the Word" in non-Christian traditions.

On a more elementary basis, the credal formulation, "I believe in one God, the Father Almighty, maker of heaven and earth," presents analogous possibilities for doctrinal dialogue. Certainly, when conversation turns to ancient creation accounts outside the biblical tradition many questions arise. But there is little question today about the shared belief of native peoples in a sovereign and transcendent Creator, a belief very likely influenced by Christianity but striking deep sympathetic traditional chords as well. In fact, native "commentators" on Christian theodicy serve to enrich it.

A second series of creedal articles pertains to the role and person of Jesus Christ. On this set of teachings there is greater need for conversation. From the traditional Christian viewpoint, it must be explained to the native peyotist that Jesus is, not the "signified" but the "signifier" (the reality behind the signs), to employ another distinction used by Siller. (Siller, 1993,6-7) To elaborate, the peyotist view of Jesus as source of healing is certainly a legitimate interpretation based on the Jesus of history as well as the belief in the Risen Christ to whom we now pray. If however, the role of Jesus becomes simply to serve as "medicine" to abet the power of peyote, then Jesus becomes a mere "signified," a means to an end, and thus dubious from a Christian point of view. In fact, peyotists who I know do not voice such a conclusion, but I cite it as a possibility. In rebuttal to it, however, is the argument of John C'Hair that all power belongs to God, and mediated through the person of Christ.

A third dimension of Christian doctrine lies not directly in the early creeds but in the tradition of the sacraments, specifically the Eucharist, in whatever ways it may be taught by any of the mainstream churches. I have in the past heard some peyotists call their medicine "our holy communion." This in itself, given the Vatican II recognition of salvific grace at work in other traditions, is valid enough. However, if it is stated as "Holy Communion" in upper case, thus becoming "the same thing" as the Eucharistic species, then there is clearly a conflict about orthodoxy. Roman Catholic thought might address this issue with the use of its tradition of "sacramentals" as opposed to "Sacraments," created elements that testify to God's work in the world. Protestant thought may find "vestiges" of the Word in these images, providing the native tradition does not for Christians replace the word and sacrament.

Fourthly, there is a rudimentary ecclesiology at issue in the peyote experience, rooted in the 1918 founding of the native American Church, coerced, as I have noted, by government pressure on peyotists. Today, as I have noted, there are many peyotists who accept only their church as the valid one for them, while others who insist, as my friend Ralph Antelope did, on their identity as mainstream Christians even while practicing native rituals. For such as these, the small local ceremony of the peyote tipi and of other practices such as the sweat lodge, might become spiritually productive cells that strengthen the people's Christian faith.

Finally, there is of course the ethical consideration based on the liceity of ingesting the mildly hallucinogenic substance, or one that is at least consciousness-altering. At the outset, it must be noted that peyote is *not* narcotic, and taken in mild doses has highly benign effects.[3] But this effect does also enter into the realm of spirituality or asceticism as well, so that it is asked whether the state of altered consciousness might be an "occasion" for authentic inspirations or visions. Given the ethical permissibility, on which there is no clear position, at least in the Catholic Church, the theologian should examine the position of Karl Rahner in his essay "Visions and Prophecies" (K. Rahner, 1964, 87-188). On the basis of Rahner's "supernatural existential" position that human experiences not sinful in themselves may share in the *de facto* "supernatural order" to which all believers belong, then this experience could be such a valid occasion for authentic spiritual communications. Conversation on this point must still be pursued, but its urgency justifies a patient and careful processual approach.

We find ourselves involved here in the specialty of systematics, which Lonergan conceives basically as a quest for understanding what we hold in faith. Systematics employs human reason in order to deepen the faith dimension, as so brilliantly exemplified over many decades by Rahner's work. To be sure, Rahner's long essay cited above does not enter into the question of chemically induced experiences, and for a study of this, one would turn, for example, to R.C. Zaehner's *Mysticism, Sacred and Profane*, which is among other things a withering rejection of Aldous Huxley's thesis that all mystical experience is essentially the same (Zaehner, 1967, x). Zaehner himself, taking his cue from Huxley, experimented with mescaline, only to find the results to be, not mystical but ludicrous (212-226). I would agree with Zaehner that all mystical experience is not the same, but did not find the effects of peyote (which contains only tiny amounts of mescaline) to be ludicrous or bizarre. This may well indicate an examination of the state of consciousness of those who use the substance, and thus their readiness for varying experiences. Could peyote then, used

3. A recent conversation with a group of Canadian native persons surfaced some comments referring to "addiction" in some peyotists. "They think they can't do without it," was the observation. Thus we must allow for the possibility of psychological as opposed to physiological addiction.

moderately under the careful supervision of spiritual leaders, be an "occasion" for spiritual inspirations?

Here one must return to Rahner's attention to visions, which are given for the conversion of all Christians. In addressing the psychological aspect of visions, and especially the problem of hallucinations or other parapsychological phenomena (Rahner 1964, 174-179), Rahner deals with a subject that has been debated ever since the earliest years of Christian mysticism, where very bizarre phenomena often made their appearance. Taking much of his commentary from Ignatius Loyola, by implication if not always explicitly, Rahner is careful to counsel Christians that all mystical experience is authentic only if it is conducive to the life of genuine holiness and virtue, in which Christians are not deceived into mistaking the means for the end, the accidental for the essential. In other words, the criteria of discernment of spirits must be applied in the topic under discussion as in the case of all spiritual phenomena.

To enter into further detailed study of Rahner's essay would extend us beyond our limits in this book. For the sake of systematic theology that might facilitate a responsible decision on chemically induced experiences, Rahner's method is helpful. In light of Rahner's theory, which relates to the earlier work of Juan Ripalda in the seventeenth century (See, for example, Perry, 1998, 442-456). any action or process that leads to more devout service of God or to holier or more virtuous life is in some way an experience of grace. One might thus suggest that dialogue about the use of peyote should function in this light and spirit. To wit, prescinding from the question of whether God has granted a vision to a peyotist, could theology conclude that his or her subsequent nobler or more virtuous life, occasioned by what happened in a meeting, is a gift of the Creator? Is there a qualitative difference between a religious experience brought on by fasting or sleeplessness, such as is practiced on some Christian pilgrimages, and the peyote experience? In fact, some traditional native leaders with whom I have talked, themselves reject peyote on these grounds, denying it an authentic place in their traditions. All of this leaves the dialogue open to further serious collaboration.

This discussion over authentic or inauthentic religious experience, then, presents us with something close to a "textbook case" of syncretism. After all the years of reflecting on and discussing native spirituality in general and peyote religion in particular, I am far from arriving at conclusive decisions about its place in the life of Christian native people. Nor should there be any rapid conclusion, especially by an outsider, no matter how friendly. This is a task for the whole Church, including specially informed aboriginal leaders in collaboration with Christian theologians. Whatever the conclusions may be, the conversation is destined to be a dramatic "communicative action" within the metaxic search for meaning in history. Again, syncretism is a *process* through which a people, so often a "besieged" people, can preserve or revitalize their cultural identity, while seeking for a deeper life of Christian faith. For the theologian, this is the path over which systematics leads eventually into communications as applied to the peyote experience.

In this application of the eighth functional specialty, we again seek the "common meaning" that constitutes community and genuine communication. We thus desire to transcend ideology and "interests" so that the gospel might be proclaimed, not as an ideology but as a freely chosen gift of God's self-communication. We are conscious, in dialogue with peyotists, that many of them choose not to embrace the Church but to remain in the native American Church, and we trust that grace reaches them through this belonging. In any case, through the methods advocated by Lonergan and Habermas, the "scandal" that causes or occasions a rejection of the invitation is at least the scandal of the gospel and not of the mission Church's sin and ineptitude. With Habermas we hope to uncover the social and cultural neuroses that have repressed authentic understanding, and, going beyond Habermas, we are aware that the symbolic dialogue takes place on the level of "myth" for all concerned, as well as on the level of critical thought. Christians, like traditional native people, also have their "myth" or story-truth, believing it to be grounded in the great historical fact of Jesus Christ.

My suggestion for communicative action in dialogue with the peyote movement as a form of syncretism embraces three dimensions: 1) "participant observation," 2) reflective conversation, and 3) praxis in liturgical form as well as in social and political solidarity. Participant observation means that one does not merely "watch" the ritual of another but in some degree shares in it. In the peyote context, that sharing involves the possibility of ingesting the substance, which is repugnant to some outsiders. Rather than push this practice at all observers, I would note that one can, by forewarning ceremonial leaders, be accepted simply as a friendly observer who does not partake. In the final analysis, this practice is even more demanding, since the all-night ritual sitting upright will be much more rigorous and possibly tedious without the mild alteration that comes with the peyote.

In any case, participation establishes the symbolic interaction of Habermas, not only in the ritual as shared by the visitor, but precisely in his or her *presence* at the meeting. I well recall the happy comments of Martha Tyler during the symbolic breakfast at the close of one meeting. This devout Catholic woman, who never missed Sunday Mass without grave reasons, expressed deep gratitude for my presence at the first meeting I attended, which had been sponsored to help her granddaughter. But there was another side to this presence: because of my slight nausea during a period of the night, I had committed the rubrical *faux pas* of lying down rather than sitting upright at attention. This mistake called forth subtle comments from one participant, as well as a gentle admonition from Frank Tyler prior to my second meeting some two years later. The beauty of that "happy fault" of mine is that it put me into the role of disciple rather than teacher; it was a minuscule case of what Frederick Crowe has called the "learning church," a Church that must learn before it can teach (Crowe, 1989, 370-384).

The ritual dimension of the dialogue may occur within rites of the mission church as well. Mission personnel have sometimes attended funerals of NAC members, generally held outdoors if at all possible, or at least in a tipi. However, on occasions when a practicing Catholic who has also prayed peyote fashion has died, peyote leaders have been invited to offer eulogy comments at the cemetery, where peyote drummers and singers may also offer a song of prayer. Peyotists appreciate this participation, since it is now part of the belief that they should seek reconciliation, healing and universal solidarity. The most obviously dramatic article of faith shared here is belief in "the life everlasting," and in the Resurrection, since the after-life is considered by native people as somehow including the whole personality.

Likewise, there is a shared belief in something like purgatory, insofar as native persons believe that sometimes a departed spirit "wanders" due to some disorder in its earthly life, until it reaches its final resting place.

On the level of reflection, no opportunity surpasses that of shared participation. Certainly, the best conversations open up as a result of my now being in a position to understand from experience and thus to concretize the theological and especially ecclesiological points discussed above. The discourse about syncretism continues, since native people are certainly in a process toward fuller appropriation of identity, whether they embrace or reject the peyote movement in their own lives. Those who consider this form of prayer to be inconsistent with their traditional native identity must further clarify that identity for themselves, while others who are Christian may decide that they have found a new form of identity within the Church. At this point in history, all of these tensions are dramatically present.

Social solidarity ensues from our entering into participation and reflection. Aboriginal peoples believe that all political action should be supported, and if possible, be accompanied by ritual. The customary forms this takes are either smoking the "peace pipe," or perhaps shared incensation, accompanied by suitable drum songs. The most rigorous sweat lodge that I have ever attended occurred when two Ojibway deacons and I attended a Sacred Fire ceremony at Sagamok Point in northern Ontario, in support of a crucial meeting in Ottawa between tribal leaders from across Canada with the federal minister of Indian Affairs, a meeting intended to take up further delicate talk about treaty rights. We were invited to join in the sweat that began about 8:00 P.M., and little expected that it would not end until after 1:00 P.M.! But this participation created a deep sense of companionship in the struggle for aboriginal rights that night.

I have noted that the peyote movement originated on the heels of the catastrophic demise of the Ghost Dance. In hindsight (which, by the way, makes it easy to blame predecessors for their mistakes), if the American government and military could have avoided the panic that ensued at news of the Ghost Dance, that ritual too might have served as a "rite of passage" for the devastated plains tribes to take a new place in the wider society with some sense of identity intact.

The peyote movement became a peaceful and more "underground" practice, after the last native fighting forces had been crushed. It has continued today as a means of reaching a deeper dimension of Turner's *communitas* for marginalized peoples. By entering into the socio-political marginalization the Church shares in this liminal condition, and is thus in a position better to help the native communities toward fuller political integration in the dominant society without their being culturally assimilated into the mainstream. In fine, the Church in its theology has taken a risk, and has become part of the struggle of threatened peoples to maintain their identities.

CONCLUSION

Our journey through the problem of syncretism has been dramatic in its sweep from the early Church to local contexts in the present. I have chosen to articulate this process under the rubric of Voegelin's Metaxy because it is a profound dimension of the human quest for meaning and order in history, politics, culture and religion. Indeed, Voegelin's five famous volumes could be interpreted as an examination of syncretic processes in search of the wholeness of truth. Such a search seems to me to express the humanistic aspirations of Erasmus when he suggested *synkretizein* to Melancthon as a metaphor for collaboration among scholars. For this reason too, I have chosen to place syncretistic experience within the dynamic of dramatic and ritual performance, relying on Victor Turner's studies, in which he and his wife, Edith, spent so many years and so much energy trying to understand the value of "passage" in human life, both social and religious.

I have tried in these pages to understand the analogies between the labors of the early "Fathers," who sought to synthesize gospel faith with Greek philosophy and Roman law, and Christian worship with elements of hellenistic myth and mystery, as well as the more ambiguous processes by which the Church became "germanized" and took on many syncretistic elements of northern Europe. I call this "more ambiguous" because so much of this influence occurred without the same kind of intellectual and spiritual guidance that was provided by the likes of Justin, Irenaeus, the Cappadocians and Augustine. By the time Anselm, Albert the Great, Bonaventure and Thomas Aquinas composed their various syntheses, many now questionable syncretisms were at work, which would eventually call for reforms enacted both by early Protestants and by the Catholic Reformation, culminating for Catholics in Vatican II. There is a gentle historical irony in the fact that, as Protestants debated on the nature of the true Reformation, "syncretism" emerged as symbolic of distortion and abandonment of principles. The irony is evident in Vatican II as well: many of its reforms, especially in liturgy, catechetics, homiletics, canon law and theories of church and state had to cope with problematic directions taken by the syncretic process, even as it set in motion forces by which new syncretic processes might implement authentic inculturation or contextualization.

In citing and discussing so many contemporary writers on syncretism, it strikes me that there is a movement away from the attack mode and towards one of "civilized discourse" about this complex phenomenon. Even if one prefers to impose a pejorative meaning onto syncretism, one might at least admit that it is a "happy fault" that can open the way to creative development. Signs of a developmental approach are evident in the work of Christian anthropologists like Luzbetak and Kraft, Catholic and Protestant respectively, in the conversations now recorded in various anthologies, and in the theological methods of Boff and Schreiter. These writers will no doubt agree with some of what I have written and disagree with other parts of it, and certainly none of them advocates a mindless embracing of syncretism. All do seem to be attentive to some distinction between the "-ism" aspect of the discussion, which distorts authentic Christianity as well as any other religion, and the "process" aspect that might lead to a responsible synthesis of gospel truth and human experience. All of these positions testify to the human search for order and solidarity.

To these contributions, this book is intended to add its own efforts toward establishing a method for dealing with syncretism both systematically and pastorally. I have chosen my own "case studies" out of some four decades of ministry among native North Americans, and have experienced some similar dynamics elsewhere on this globe that is so rapidly becoming a village. It is my hope that this book might contribute to the creation of a village that expresses the best in village life—hospitality and conversation, and not the worst, such as conflict and manipulation. I realize that this village seems destined to be pluralistic, and that all dialogue must accept the fact of a historical pluralism, certainly of cultures, (Who would want that otherwise?) and in the historical experience of religion. As a follower and preacher of the gospel of Christ, I have sought to offer that "good news" without undue scandal to all who would accept it. To those who do not accept it, I offer my understanding of its moral and spiritual values to accompany their own in our "communicative action" that must constitute our life in the Metaxy. Given that we are still in the Metaxy, no treatment of so complex a reality as syncretism can be "conclusive." But it is my hope that the foregoing has added some clarity and suggested some creative praxis. Might we not symbolize syncretism in the parable of the talents, so that it becomes an investment that the Householder has entrusted to us, and with which we are assigned to "do business"?

APPENDIX 1
CHRISTIAN VIEWS OF SYNCRETISM

ORIGINS OF THE WORD AS A SOLUTION
RATHER THAN A PROBLEM

The Cretans did not have a good press in Christian sources. St. Paul, or a Pauline writer, admonishing presbyters to adhere to sound teaching and warning about false teachers in the Jewish community, singles out false teachers in Crete as his bad example by quoting the Cretan poet Epimenides: "Cretans have ever been liars, beasts, and lazy gluttons" (Titus, 1:12). Whatever the heresy was in question in Crete, it seems that the verb "to cretize" was equated with lying, and thus may have more than a coincidental relation with the eventual usage of the related verb "to syncretize" as equivalent to heresy. Or, it may be that Plutarch, to whom the word "syncretize" was connected, may have been using the islanders, for all their faults, as his example of people who could achieve a healthy if pragmatic kind of harmony among their own tribes by uniting against a common external enemy. Thus, the contemporary anthropologists, Stewart and Shaw (1994,3-4) refer readers to a discussion by Plutarch, in his *Peri Philadelphias* (On Fraternal Love) of the ability of Cretans to join forces and thus become "brothers" in spite of differences, in order to fight a common enemy (much as in the case of the Crusades noted in my introduction). These writers observe further that Plutarch may have been punning on the word *synkrasis* (a mixture), although Rudolph thinks that the "mixture" interpretation came after the Reformation (Rudolph, 1979,196). A reading of the Greek text seems clearly to indicate that Plutarch interpreted the Cretans to be referring directly to their own pragmatic ability to strike a mutually useful truce among their often hostile clans, and thus at least to *behave* as "brothers." They named this practice after themselves—*synkretismos*—"uniting Cretans" (see Paton et. al, 1972, 249-250).

The word "syncretism" did not make its way into Christian literature until Erasmus chose to employ it, fittingly enough, as a defense policy for humanists. Writing to Philip Melancthon in 1519, he commiserates with the future Reformation father, who seems to have been suffering a calumniation of some kind by an unnamed person. Since Melancthon seems to have brought up some particular opinion in the dispute, Erasmus writes that "those especially who cherish the holy things of the Muses" should proceed carefully to follow all that is "right, true, fitting and honest" (Allen and Allen, 1913, 539-540). Then Erasmus writes, "You can see with what great hatred they conspire against good letters (humane learning). Thus, it is fitting that we should *synkretizein*. Union of hearts (concordia) is a mighty wall of strength" (540).

There have been a few comments over the years as to what the Dutch humanist meant: he may have been advocating a union of Christian theology and humanistic studies, (Stewart and Shaw, 4) or he may simply have been urging his fellow scholar to be his ally against a common foe. In any case, this little letter is hardly an indication of the storm that would swirl around the term that he was using perhaps simply as a rhetorical device.

André Droogers (Gort et al., 1989,9) writes of the way in which seventeenth century Protestant writers gave the term a negative meaning, but does not oblige us with any data on this point. One does however find considerably more help in two articles from different generations. The first is found in the article by James Moffatt in *Hasting's Encyclopedia of Religion and Ethics* (1922, 155). Moffatt discusses how Zwingli first, then G. Calixtus, in the first half of the seventeenth century sought to unite the churches of the Protestant Reformation in common cause against Rome, and others of similar irenic mentality even urged dialogue with Rome in the name of common Christianity. Over a half-century later, Kurt Rudolph describes further detail on the late sixteenth and seventeenth century "syncretists" (Rudolph, 1979,195-196). But the demonization of the term as meaning crude hybridism was to carry over into the nineteenth and eventually the twentieth centuries.

SYNCRETISM AS UNPRINCIPLED COMMINGLING

As Carsten Colpe has written, the negative view of syncretism as haphazard mixing appeared in the religious philosophy of Hermann Usener, who called it a kind of *Religionsmischerei* ("religious mishmash"), as opposed to a more neutral related word, *Mischung* ("mixture") (Eliade, 1987, XIV, 218). Commenting on the work of the Stoic philosophers in their efforts to emerge from the confusion of polytheism into the pure experience of the divine power in the Universal Spirit (*Weltgeist*), he notes how early Christian theologians found stoicism a "point of contact" (*Anknüpfungspunkt*) with hellenistic philosophy (Usener, 1929, 337). But he then adds, "On the other hand, the enlightened heathen felt himself so in agreement with Christians on the essential point that he (she) saw no reason for conversion" (Glaubenswechsel) (Usener, 1929, 339). Many evangelicals would see this comment as affirming the uselessness of harmonizing efforts. However, Usener also commented further: "Syncretism, which seems to us a characterless, frivolous and repugnant falsification of the faith of our fathers, is an important transitional stage in the history of religions. It was the preparatory school for the belief in the One God" (340). This statement might admit of a more positive meaning of syncretism as having a purpose within the development of religious interpretation, and thus not be entirely opposed to the mind of God. This is the direction taken by some contemporary theologians. In the early years of the twentieth century, the challenge of syncretism found a sophisticated interpreter in Adolf Harnack, who accepted the fact that early Christianity and even late Judaism were already syncretistic. Harnack, like Usener, considered syncretism to be already present in Judaism, and soon to become an "internal condition" in the expansion of the Christian movement, as an aspiration toward the essential unity of humankind. For Harnack, syncretism was a phenomenon that Christianity had to reckon with in order to simplify and cleanse itself (Harnack, 1904, 37-39). He considered even the Nicene Creed to be a syncretism of the faith with hellenistic philosophy, through which Christianity had to pass to free itself from Jewish soil (74). In terminology that would become famous in our time, Harnack maintained that Christianity would have to distinguish between its own "kernel" and the "husk" enclosing it (74). Thus did he recommend that the purification of Christian syncretism must proceed via the great reduction to the "essence of Christianity": belief in the one living God, in Jesus as savior and judge, in the Resurrection, and in the self-discipline of the higher morality (116).

In a far more radically evangelical sweep, Hendrik Kraemer, in his famous response to the "Hocking Report," would deal with syncretism as an abuse to be purged, not by reduction to central elements, but to the revelation found in "biblical realism" (Kraemer, 1961, 83 and *passim*). Christianity, as the one religion of the true revelation, must take an adversarial stance against all other religious forms, since "Every religion is a living, indivisible unity"(135). Each is "a total religious apprehension, with which there is no "point of contact"" (300). Not only must Christianity resist all the great "world religions" as forms of "self-asserting human vitalism"; it must also resist syncretism, which Kraemer called "a primitive apprehension of existence" (203). While the Church should consider the values of indigenous forms insofar as they might express the "eternal essence" of Christianity, there must be no harmonizing or accommodation (200-211). He would only fortify his position in his later volume, *Religions and the Christian Faith*, even though it engaged some reconsideration of points in his earlier volume.   The point of departure for the contemporary Christian "power encounter" with syncretism is, at least arguably, W. A. Visser 't Hooft's *No Other Name* (Visser 't Hooft, 1963). This small book is a carefully wrought testimony on behalf of the gospel's universality and is intended as a Christian alternative to syncretism. Visser 't Hooft employs the Oxford English Dictionary's definition in the very frontispiece of the book: "...attempted union or reconciliation of diverse or opposite tenets or practices, especially in philosophy of religion" (Frontispiece). Over against this he sets the words of Acts 4:10: "There is no other name under heaven by which we must be saved" than that of Jesus Christ. Syncretism, says the author, being careful to distinguish it from faithful "translation" of the gospel, is more dangerous than atheism, because it seems to be so inevitable (10-11). Given his conviction as to the demonic character of syncretism, the author's argument from this point follows an irrefutable logic, rejecting the claims of syncretists of all the great religions, Christian, Islamic, Buddhist and Hindu, that they could create a "world religion" free of any previous identity. This he calls "a revolt against the uniqueness of revelation in history" (48). Therefore, the very foundation of a power encounter with syncretism is the New Testament itself, which carefully avoids certain hellenistic terms such as *eros, enthousiasmos,* and *mythos,* while appropriating and redefining—in fact, transforming—other words like *kyrios, logos, soter, euangelion* and *gnosis,* which represent a true *Heilsgeschichte* Christology, and thus undergo a profound change in meaning (73). Visser t'Hooft appreciates the universal appeal of syncretism: the human soul is more *naturaliter syncretistica* than it is "naturally Christian" (83). Since, then, it is such a constant and plausible temptation, how must Christian theology deal with it? First, Christian theologians must make a careful distinction between religion and culture, given that cultural synthesis is indeed inevitable. Second, none of the great religions should denigrate the others by giving in to the idea of one great world religion; this is not the way of true ecumenism (88).

There are voices on the "left" in this discussion that also take the polemical approach to syncretism. Two of the best known to missiologists are Taiwanese Protestant C.S. Song, and the Camerounian Catholic Fabian Eboussi Boulaga. One must ask here why each of these takes pains to bring up syncretism and to dismiss it, however much each one seems to desire an Asian or African transformation.

Song's position, which he may perhaps be said to raise implicitly in later works, is stated in one of his earliest books, *Christian Mission in Reconstruction.* At first he employs the word in an effort to critique theologians who fear to introduce "the particular" into their "universal" message: "But those who are engaged in Christian mission have often been hesitant to affirm this for fear of syncretism" (Song, 1977, 106). He devotes a later chapter to syncretism, which he sets at the opposite end of a spectrum beginning with dogmatism (174ff.). Dogmatism is the basically Eurocentric attitude towards theological interpretation, which absolutizes European culture. However, "the so-called syncretism" is also a search for the absolute, but its quest is for solutions that gather in all of the elements of diverse religions into one new religion. The wrongheadedness of syncretism for Song is not in the recognition of diverse claims, but in its attempt "to incorporate into the body of the Christian faith similar teachings and beliefs that happen to be found in other religions" (179).

Eboussi's argument is similar to Song's, though expressed in the complex dialectic so typical of this theologian. For him, syncretism occurs when people assume that Christianity is hereditary; it is thus a religious phenomenon that occurs among people who have not yet become adequately conscious of their historicity, and so remain prisoners of a substantial corruption of their own reality and that of others. Seeking solutions to the loss of cultural identity they develop syncretistic solutions (Eboussi, 1981, 70-71). This leads to "... an emulsion of trifles and vacuities ... (which) recoils before the Paschal requirement of losing all in order to save one's life, or dying in order to rise again and enter into glory" (71-72).

CONTEMPORARY POSITIONS: THE "POWER ENCOUNTER"

In his 1987 *Introduction to Missiology*, the late Alan Tippett dismisses syncretism as an evil thirty-two times, without ever defining his use of the term. Thus, when St. Paul denounced *koinonia ton daimonion* (fellowship with demons) among the Corinthians (1 Cor.10-19-21), he was attacking syncretism (Tippett, 1987, 41). Syncretism is a danger in local church-growth (47), a form of "backsliding" (278), a disloyal co-existence with non-Christian forms (83), a partner with "universalism" against authentic mission (109), a type of neo-paganism (147) or "christopaganism" manifested in the cult of Guadalupe, for example, though Tippett leaves this cult unnamed (173). It is a compromise with animism that must be replaced with "functional substitutes" that are congenial to the gospel (187,188, 192). An evil "rife since apostolic times" (361), it is characteristic of "nativistic movements" (passim), and a compromise with pagan rites, while it likewise joins with modern rationalization to become a temptation to be confronted by the Church through "power encounters."

Two of Tippett's American contemporaries are the Protestant Charles Kraft and the Catholic Louis Luzbetak, both of whom share

Tippett's negative interpretation but who make efforts to better define and research the phenomenon, understanding it as a more processual reality. Kraft improves on Tippett's work in two ways especially; 1) by carefully describing syncretism as a cultural fact, and 2) by making some creative theological distinctions. To do this, Kraft focuses on forms and meanings. Thus he writes, "When old forms are used in new ways, the tendency is for people to interpret them as if they still carry the older meanings. This results in syncretism. The meaning problem must be constantly confronted with scriptural teaching concerning what the Christian meanings are intended to be" (Kraft, 1996, 213).

Kraft defines syncretism as "...the mixing of Christian meanings with pagan meanings in such a way that the result is not really Christian, though it may on the surface look like Christianity" (260). There is reason to fear this, but there is no reason to fear taking risks. Consequently, Kraft distinguishes between two types of syncretism: 1). "when the receiving peoples retain many of their own practices with their indigenous meanings and mix them with practices that look Christian," and 2) "...when they adopt foreign (Christian) forms wholesale but retain their own meanings" (260). Kraft wisely understands this phenomenon to be a result of foreign pressure. To remedy it he goes on later to dismiss the theory by which some equate syncretism and contextualization, admitting that many times "locals" may be spiritually right! (375-379) Local forms are not necessarily ways in which Satan may have bound them to his own purposes, though they may be such. Thus, as Gregory I had written, the focus should be, not on destroying the forms but in breaking Satanic power over them (313). "Culture" he writes, "is culture. Culture is not the enemy. The enemy is the enemy. Let's oppose the right enemy, not the wrong one" (328).

Luzbetak studies syncretism under the heading of "Christo-paganism" as well as "dual religious systems" (Luzbetak, 1989, 360-373). He contributes another helpful distinction between an anthropologist's understanding and that of Christian missiology. Thus, "Syncretism is understood in anthropology as any synthesis of two or more culturally diverse beliefs or practices, especially if of a religious character" (360). Thus, the basic interest for anthropologists is not "religion" or "theology" but culture, while in missiology the term involves Christian theology, so that syncretism "may be narrowly defined as any theologically untenable amalgam" (360).

Luzbetak admits that syncretism, while untenable in theology, is unavoidable as an expression of a people's central values, which demand our respect (360). To drive this point home, he discusses various forms of nativist syncretisms, but juxtaposes them to the even more dangerous "western" or European syncretisms such as hedonism, scientism, positivism, individualism, commercialism and materialism, to mention a few (366). He also reminds readers that syncretism is conspicuous in the history of Israel, even with its fierce devotion to the one God. Thus, in the labor of preaching the Gospel, syncretism will always be with us: "A syncretism-free Church is an eschatological hope, not a reality," for the pilgrim Church (369).

SYNCRETISM AS A METAXIC DIALOGUE

Dialogue with syncretism, however we may interpret it, should not be confused with syncretism itself; in fact, syncretism can be interpreted as a form of dialogue. Perhaps the best known of modern writers to look positively upon the definition of syncretism was the American philosopher and churchman, William Ernest Hocking, who led the team of laypersons on a famous tour of Protestant missions in the late 1920s and early 1930s. One object of his attack was the attitude of exclusivism, against which he advocated what he called "the way of synthesis" (Hocking, 1940, 183), for which he gave three criteria: individuality, organic unity, and consistency. Every religion, while not complete in itself, must have its own distinct individuality in order to be able to adopt elements from other religions. But the process of borrowing can then lead to a higher organic unity: " What is added must not remain extraneous, like an ornament or a piece of baggage, but must become a part of the organism of the living religion" (183). There must however be a consistency in such organic unity, so that integrity of the religion is not destroyed.

Responding to the Kraemer camp, Hocking observed: "In the fear of syncretism, we have a justified, but on the whole timorous attitude to alien religions: it shows a smallness of faith in what one has which, at any point, tends to deprive of sustenance that very religion it seeks so sedulously to preserve" (186). Basically, there are other elements in other religions that belong to ours, if we become capable of adopting them. This would become the premise of Hocking's "way of reconception," typically enough a form of idealist theology that would permit of a dynamic construction of a new religious reality out of the union of two more basic realities. Wolfhardt Pannenberg, writing in the late 1960s (Pannenberg, 1971), was deeply concerned with one of the issues that always involves a discussion of syncretism: the "ultimacy" of the Christian revelation understood as a part of the universal history of religion (69). This led him into a discussion of the meaning of syncretism, a word which he believes should be dealt with more objectively and free from previous biases that have clouded the discussion (85-86). Pannenberg does not renounce his faith in the ultimacy of the Christian revelation, but he notes that the quest for absolute purity in a religion and total freedom from any forms of integration are hardly possible—an argument he uses in discussing the very idea of God in the Old Testament (87). In a footnote to this observation, he defends his belief that any syncretic process presupposes an integrating principle prior to the different elements under consideration. Thus, in Hellenistic philosophy it was the *Logos*; in Christianity it is Jesus Christ and his redemptive death and resurrection. Given this, Pannenberg could say, "The fact that Christianity is syncretistic in an unusual degree thus expresses not a weakness but the unique strength of Christianity" (87-88). It affords the greatest example of assimilative power.

The late Indian theologian M.M. Thomas takes up Pannenberg's basic approach in a 1985 article. Thomas agrees with Hendrik Kraemer's "main emphasis" on the centrality of Christ, even while "going beyond" Kraemer (Thomas, 1985, 388). He agrees with Kraemer's emphasis on the need for "adaptation," defending Kraemer against critics who accuse him of cultural arrogance or narrowness. Where Thomas differs with Kraemer is on the latter's negative definition of syncretism and his total rejection of it. Instead, Thomas argues " the case for syncretism of a kind," because he correctly sees how so many church persons took up this negative definition in order to condemn all forms of adaptation. Thomas shrewdly points out that Kraemer's rejection of the word had the very opposite effect to that intended by Kraemer in his defense of cultural adaptation (389).

Thomas discusses the ongoing competition (though he does not use the word) among all the religions to be the integrating dynamic spoken of by Pannenberg. Each of these systems is grounded in a living faith, and each must be allowed its say in any conversation. But Christianity, for Thomas, while it must listen to proposals from the other religions, also has the opportunity to let Jesus Christ "break down the wall of partition between Christians and others" (391). Taking issue with Kramer, he writes

> In this sense the unintegrated mixtures of religions, ideological and cultural elements, which Kraemer calls syncretistic, are inevitable; they are legitimate for the Christian and for the church so long as they are not seen as a goal in themselves but indicate a movement towards a new integration or adaptation based in Christian fundamentals (392).

This hope for long-range integration reflects the remark of Jürgen Moltmann, "The syncretism which dissolves Christian identity only comes about if people lose sight of the future, to which Christianity is called" (Moltmann, 1977, 163).

The Brazilian Leonardo Boff has most positively embraced the phenomenon of syncretism. In his famous and controversial book, *Church: Charism and Power*, Boff includes a chapter entitled "In Favor of Syncretism: The Catholicity of Catholicism." Boff sees the syncretic process as a sign of the "courage for incarnation" (Boff, 1986, 89), and as "an acceptance of heterogeneous elements and their subsequent integration within the criteria of a specifically Catholic ethos... a Catholicism whose present reality and future destiny are determined by its capacity to syncretize" (89). Boff quickly shifts the point of observation away from privileged places into a context of conflicts and challenges where Catholicism is seen as a living reality and thus open to other elements.[1] Boff thus seeks to snatch the power of defi-

---

1. For a similar viewpoint from a similar perspective, see Vergilio Elizondo's positive attitude towards syncretism in his *Guadalupe: Mother of the New Creation* (Elizondo, 1997, 126-127). A like sense of the value of the process for oppressed peoples seems to motivate David Carrasco's definition of syncretism: "The complex process by

nition away from those who have always feared it, "the defenders of theological and institutional knowledge," among whom he includes Visser 't Hooft and even the Second Vatican Council (89-90).

Boff examines syncretism under six possible rubrics: addition, accommodation, mixture, agreement, translation and adaptation. As addition, syncretism takes place only in the personal experience of a believer "whose own diffused and undefined religiosity" values all kinds of experiences without reflecting on their validity—clearly, syncretism in the pejorative sense, lacking a specific identity. Accommodation occurs "when the religion of the dominated people is adapted to the religion of those who dominate, but as a means of survival or as part of a strategy for resistance" (90). Syncretism as mixture is a tautology, of course, both since the word itself signifies a "mixture" as Boff notes (178-179). and because all religions feature some kinds of mixing. Actually, it does not seem much different from syncretistic addition, as the practice of the Greeks and Romans shows in their absorption of near eastern elements. For Boff, this too is equated with dilution and confusion, without any unity other than what occurs in the inner life of each practitioner, "believers who feel the power of so many different deities" (90). Differing from this type, by reason of various believers coming together to join different paths to the divine reality, is the phenomenon of syncretism by agreement. Boff here agrees with other authors, Kraemer and Visser 't Hooft especially, that such agreement loses all sense of unique identity, as well as any belief in a unique revelation. He calls this type superficial and lacking in organic wholeness.

The last two categories embrace the positive aspects of syncretism. Translation is the practice by which one religion uses the categories, cultural expressions and traditions of another religion to communicate and translate its own essential message, choosing only the compatible elements of the foreign religion. This is a process followed by all universal religions. Adaptation is the form of syncretism that Boff favors, understanding the term to mean what most theologians today mean by inculturation. Adaptation is a long, almost impercep-

which rituals, beliefs and symbols from different religions are combined into new meanings. Syncretism is most clearly represented in ritual performances that enable people to locate themselves within a new world of meaning" (Carrasco, 1990, 169).

tible process in the development of religion; it is a more deeply *intentional* process of interpretation and assimilation that realizes that it too will trigger crises and uncertainty. Boff's value for our discussion lies in his advocacy for the marginalized in their struggles for identity, which lead them to create syncretistic forms of religion.

Another theologian who approaches the theme, in a similar if more reserved fashion, is Robert Schreiter. In his celebrated *Constructing Local Theologies*, he too assumes the negative approach to syncretism as a dilution and loss of the message in a local context (Schreiter, 1985, 102). But he then shrewdly suggests drawing back from the possibilities of syncretism in order to deal with the discontinuity that may arise in any local theology. In his concluding section, Schreiter devotes space to understanding and dealing with syncretism.

In his later book, *The New Catholicity*, Schreiter devotes a chapter to the relationship between syncretism and religious identity in the "re-encoding" of messages, and observes that probably syncretic and synthetic processes are equivalent (Schreiter, 1997, 71). For Schreiter, a deeper study of the processes will lead to a more authentic catholicity for Christianity. Thus, without calling for an uncritical acceptance of this concept, he simply argues that the conversation must continue, especially in view of so many issues around the relationships between religion and cultural identity.

I conclude discussion of positive approaches to syncretism with a necessarily brief description of a remarkable symposium held in Germany under the guidance of Hermann Siller (Siller, 1991).[2] The anthology is most perceptively called *Suchbewegungen* ("search-movements"), since the tone of the entire work emphasizes that syncretism is a tensive historical movement—an exercise of the Metaxy, as I have suggested. It is unique among anthologies, since it was composed with the precise intention of addressing issues within the Christian fold, as its subtitle suggests: "Cultural Identity and Ecclesial Confession." Even more striking is the manner in which these authors, apparently *because* they are professing Christians, embrace syncretic reality as a value within the passage of human experience.

---

2. I am indebted to Professor Schreiter for calling my attention to this excellent study.

Especially valuable in relation to any attempt to develop a theology of syncretism are the following points in the collection.

1) So many, if not all, syncretic religious developments take place among marginalized peoples, the "periphery" (Siller, in Siller, 1991, 1—17). This means that mainline church dialogue with syncretism necessarily includes dialogue with the "troubled" and "threatened" cultures (Siller, in Siller, 1991, 174—184). It is for such peoples as these that syncretism is a "solution" to their concern for maintenance of identity, while for the more powerful and mainstream communities with much privilege to lose it is a "problem." This fact makes patient and long-term dialogue essential.

2) All the essays in this volume argue for the involvement of local communities and especially their spiritual leaders in any discernment of direction for mission. Several writers employ the term *bricolage* ("puttering") (taken from C. Levi-Strauss) to describe the function of local leaders who create rituals and new ideas that serve for the preservation of cultural identity. These *bricoleurs* construct new "collages" that symbolize cultural wholeness (Greverus, in Siller, 1991, 18–30). This also means that foreign church representatives must become deeply informed about local "folk religions" (Ahrens, in Siller, 1991, 62–83; Gesch, 84-94).

3) Dialogue with tribal or folk religions always demands attention to their deep sense of community, with its stress on action rather than doctrine (Sundermeier, in Siller, 1991, 95–105). If any intellectual process is to be pursued, then the study of myth, with its emphasis on a people's story rather than any forms of doctrine, must figure prominently (D'Sa, in Siller, 1991, 17–129). Within this dialogue, the local culture takes on the "commentator" role emphasized by communications theory, while the mainstream religion consents to be the "commentandum," or the one subject to interpretation. This creates a sharing of the passive and active roles in dialogue.

4) Finally, a creative (but dense!) development of hegelian thought employs the idea of the interchange of "subject and predicate" as a means of discerning the legitimacy of a syncretic practice or idea in relation to Christian doctrine (May, in Siller, 1991, 185—192). Thus, if a structure, concept or thought is an authentic representation of Jesus Christ, this could point to a legitimate form of syncretism. As

an example, not used by May, the inclusion of a sacred pipe within Amerindian Christian liturgies to symbolize Christ may serve as an enrichment of the event, since the pipe has become a "predicate" of the subject Christ. If the pipe symbolism takes over the role of "subject," with Christ then becoming a mere symbol of the local religion, syncretism has lost its authenticity. Siller wisely allows that there is need here for a fair analysis of *who* is to have "power" in such determinations! In fine, while this symposium leaves many grave problems for theology, it represents perhaps the most creative effort to date to deal with it.

APPENDIX 2
NON-CONFESSIONAL VIEWS
OF SYNCRETISM

We can ill afford to neglect examining the work of historians and phenomenologists of religion as they attempt to "understand" this terribly complex phenomenon.[1] In his great *Religion in Essence and Manifestation*, Gerardus Van der Leeuw carefully maintains his own phenomenological "restraint" (*epoché*) in dealing with syncretism. First he identifies syncretism with "the process leading repeatedly from polydaimonism to polytheism" (Van der Leeuw, 1963, 169). In a passage that predates later less hostile views of syncretism, he states, "In the development of cultures man finds the universe becoming steadily smaller; his world is no longer limited to his own village, but extends to a number of such communities linked together by manifold connections, and ultimately to a province, a state, to neighboring states" (169).

Out of such extensions arises a new understanding between one's own and foreign powers, and thus a movement toward a "Pantheon" of deities. But the movement develops into a quest (discussed earlier by Usener) for one overarching deity. This leads Van der Leeuw to contextualize the relations between missions and syncretism within the phenomena of all historically developing religions: "Every religion, therefore, has its own previous history and is to a certain extent a 'syncretism'" (609). Christianity and Islam are not exempt from such a process in their historical dynamism. Religions thus borrow forms from other religions and subject them to "transposition" (*Verschiebung*), which is "...the variation of the significance of any phenomenon, occurring in the dynamic of religions, while its form remains quite unaltered" (610-611).

1. For an excellent recent survey of all the following theorists, as well as of the entire field up to his time of writing, see Kurt Rudolph's essay. (Rudolph, 1979)

Another element to be accepted as proper to syncretism is its "ambiguity." This is the argument of an article published in 1971 by Michael Pye. Discussing J.H. Kamstra's assertion that even Hendrik Kraemer's "pure" Christianity is also syncretistic, and examining Kamstra's efforts at a more phenomenological and thus non-judgmental approach, Pye takes issue with one of Kamstra's major points—that syncretism is a kind of alienation within a religion when it develops or takes on foreign elements. For Pye, syncretism is not always about alienation from within, but may occur as a result of a religion moving "towards without" and thus *voluntarily* embracing syncretic processes (Pye, 1971, 86-87). This leads Pye, in agreement with Kamstra's call for a partnership between phenomenology and theology, to suggest that theologians recognize the syncretic processes *within* the faiths they represent, as well as the relations they have toward other religions. Pye's recognition of syncretism calls for a theology of "ambiguity" as a criterion for describing the phenomenon, which is "a natural *moving* aspect of major religious traditions" (92). The theologian, then, must be prepared to deal with the syncretisms in his/ her tradition as temporary processes in the dynamics of authentic development. Thus, we move into our examination of phenomenological scholars by means of Pye's definition of syncretism as "...the temporary ambiguous coexistence of elements from divers religions and other contexts within a coherent religious pattern" (93).

James Moffatt (Hastings, 1922, 155-157), writing in the early part of the twentieth century, discusses the early origins of the term in Plutarch and later in Erasmus and the first Protestants who used it. He describes how those Protestant church leaders came to see syncretism as "hybridization" rather than authentic harmony. In comparative religion, however, Moffatt notes, scholars look upon syncretistic processes as ways in which hitherto warring tribes or nations might approach higher forms of agreement by uniting their practices and fusing their gods (*theocrasia*). Moffatt also points out that both Judaism and Christianity were wary of such blending from the beginning, and that their proponents (e.g., Philo for the Jews) sought, not a blending, but a reinterpretation of their faiths in new terms, and thus an *absorption* of gentile elements.

Writing in Mircea Eliade's *Encyclopedia of Religion* more than a half century later, Carsten Colpe (Eliade, 1987, XII, 218-227) extends the investigation into the term by suggesting how anthropologists and other social scientists might employ it. He recommends the "neutrality" of which we have spoken, in order to study the functional uses of syncretism. Colpe thus approaches syncretism by seeking to render it as an "explanatory category" for providing "a socio-psychological clarification of a readiness for the balancing, subordination, superordination, and unification of truth" (219). To engage the process, scholars must develop an interpretation of the term in the here-and-now, rather than clinging to meanings given it in its earlier history. Colpe goes on here to develop a typology under two headings: the relations between complex wholes of irreducible values, and the relations between *particular components* of those wholes and how they might be linked. Syncretism may thus be either a relatively static state, or it may be a process; the role of research is to determine into which category a given syncretic phenomenon belongs.

PHENOMENOLOGICAL TREATMENTS OF SYNCRETISM

Antiquity

Wisely, scholars seem to have refrained from seeking to isolate "pure" ancient religions; they see even those studies of pre-Christian experience as studies in syncretism, revealing valuable insights for contemporary study. Thus, for example, ancient Chinese religion was such a perfect synthesis of what today we call culture and religion, that no one can really distinguish one from the other. One author in a symposium during the late 1960s (Sjöholm in Hartmann, 1969, 110-127), finds culture and religion to be virtually equated in ancient China. And to the west, in the "fertile crescent," (Kapelrud, in Hartmann, 1969, 112-170), the prophetic protests against idolatry were a later development in Israel, after the Chosen People had long since migrated peacefully into the "promised land." Another scholar, writing in another anthology, is in agreement with this observation (Ahlstrom in Pearson, 1975, 1-19), describing the many ways in which

Judaism adopted Canaanite symbols into its own system of worship and general culture.

According to another writer, however, the religious elements that the incoming Hebrews encountered were already heavily syncretistic, rather than purely autochthonous (J. Van Dijk, in Hartmann, 1969, 171-206). Prehistoric evidence reveals creation myths describing the separation of water and dry land (175-178), and the semitic peoples incorporated versions of this into their own mythology. The same author points out the deeply political motivation behind this syncretism, as for example, Sargon using religious amalgams to unite his subjects (179).

Further political implications in religious syncretism appear in the relations between ancient Israel and Iran in the Parthian period. According to Geo Widengren (Pearson, 1971, 85-129), Jews and Parthians united ("syncretized") in their hatred of Rome, resulting in such phenomena as an amalgamated collection of art in the synagogues (94), and the growth of "apocalyptic" judgment themes, with the world becoming increasingly a battleground between good and evil, and history "a drama advancing toward a climax, the final judgment" (129). Out of such unions and crises, according to Birger Pearson (Pearson, 1971, 85-129, 205-222), a "new hermeneutic" arose that would burgeon into a dramatic development of pre-Christian Gnosticism—that is, as we shall see below, the syncretism against which New Testament theology seems to contend so often and vigorously.

Similar processes occurred as well in the world of the Greeks (Bergman in Hartmann, 1969, 207-227). Herodotus seems to have believed that all the Greek gods originated in Egypt, although there is some obscurity around how they related the names of deities to the forms they took (216). One Graeco-Egyptian "point of contact" describes how Hercules was appointed general by Osiris, whose two sons were named Anubis and Makedon (221-222). In general, the article concludes, it was quite acceptable to adopt foreign names for local deities (224). One significant question arising from this account pertains to the crucial issue of who had the "power" to absorb the other's deities.

In another study of biblical presuppositions for and against syncretism, the writer (Wessels in Gort, 1989, 52-65) describes a "theomachy" that seems to have been the situation of Israel's sojourn in Canaan. The high god El of the Canaanites was eventually absorbed by the Hebrew Yahweh, as was Baal originally, even though Baal was finally reduced to a defeated fertility god by Elijah and Hosea. (58) This latter deity even entered into a symbolic fertility union with a Canaanite harlot in order to demonstrate Yahweh's redeeming power (60). The conclusion from this study is that Israel was culturally and religiously syncretistic, but that the one God overcame all opposition by "transforming" the other gods into subjected deities (62).

The Middle Ages

From the few examples cited above, one can gain some degree of awareness of the syncretistic amalgam into which Christianity was born. Indeed, one of the earliest gnostic sects was formed by the Macedonians in order to defeat early Syrian Christianity and to do battle with Jesus (Segelberg in Hartmann, 1969, 228-239).

Religious developments in Scandinavia from the time of the first Christian missions reveal the type of syncretism that, as Van der Leeuw points out, accompanies missions, especially whenever there is a severe curb on communications. Typical of the encounter between missionaries and tribal societies is the mingling of nomadic Lapp traditions with those of the southern Scandinavian nordic tribes who had embraced Christianity in the seventh century (Nordland in Hartmann, 1969, 66-99). Syncretism also appears in folk medicine for such events as pregnancy and childbirth, where elements of primal taboo are combined with the doctrine of original sin. A defective child was thus seen as being the result of a combination of both ideas (Weiser-All in Hartmann, 1969, 100-109). Such amalgams have continued into the present day through the medium of modern literature (Strom, in Hartmann, 1969, 240-262). In fact, a great deal of Germanic religious history combines Finnish, Icelandic, Indo-German and Irish elements. Christian eschatology as expressed in these lands draws both on the Christian tradition and on the *Götter-dammerung* of nordic saga. The two figures of Christ and Longinus are mingled with those of Achilles and Paris. Elsewhere Christ is garbed in "heathen dress" as a Nordic hero, Balder, who one tenth century poet used as a kind of "pedagogue" leading his people to Christ (247). In all, within medieval Germanic Christianity different gods became substitute names for the devil. It is clear how deeply this fascinating mixture figures in our examination of developments of Christianity in northern Europe.

Synchronous with the above north European developments were the phenomena occurring in pre-contact and then in post-contact Mesoamerica, as described by David Carrasco (1990), who begins his study with the arrival of the fifteenth century Franciscans in the "New World," and their discovery of the religions of the Mayas and Aztecs—religions focusing primarily on world order and renewal of their societies. In a subdued but graphic description, Carrasco narrates the grim conflict between two cultures that emphasized both combat and conquest as well as high and elaborate sacrificial ritual concepts. Even more among the Maya did the ancient religion mingle with the new Christian one in the form of pilgrimages, creation myths, and the celebration of the aboriginal feasts of the dead in tandem with the feasts of All Saints and All Souls. Among the Aztecs, the earth goddess Tonantzin was eventually "homologized" with the Virgin of Guadalupe (135), while Santiago (St. James) became the fertility deity among the Mayas (147).

Contemporary Phenomena

If there is any comparative religion concept that is universal, none can be more universal than syncretism, especially as it occurs in the fusion of tribal religion and Christianity. In the same symposium at Abo, Sweden (Hartmann, 1969), several essays focus on the mixing of Christian and pagan elements. One lecture, perhaps inclined to overgeneralize, describes the syncretistic character of the North American version of the Peyote Religion, in which the Great Spirit is homologized to the Christian God, and the various culture heroes are likened to Jesus Christ (Ringgren in Hartmann, 1969, 1-14). Another focusing on North American aboriginal cultures touches on the "Sun Dance" of the Wind River Shoshones (Hultktrantz, 1969, 15-40). This ritual is a case study of the political and social functions of syncretism, a point also brought out by Joseph Jorgensen (1972) and Dmitri Shimkin (1953) before him. This version was transmitted to the Crow people of southern Montana in 1941 by spiritual leader John Trujero at the request of Crow leader William Big Day, whose tribe had lost its original Sun Dance (see Crummett, 1993).

Similar syncretisms occur in Africa, as an article on Tanzania describes (Petterson in Hartmann, 1969, 41-65). As is generally true in sub-Saharan Africa, the Sonjo of Tanzania claim a primitive monotheism, as well as a myth of the dying and rising culture hero who will reward all the faithful. On the other hand, the god here is not seen as explicitly the creator, and Africans do not have a close relationship with their tribal supreme deities. This article could only speculate on the degree to which contemporary Christian belief is influenced by this interface between the aboriginal and the Christian.

Japan also has a prominent example of syncretistic outgrowths of both Buddhism and Christianity (Thomsen in Hartmann, 1969, 128-136). Here a pragmatic approach to religion leads to diverse syncretistic usages and questions of religious identity. This author departs briefly from "pure" phenomenology to ask a missiological question: Can Christianity in Japan be renewed by the inclusion of such elements as Zen prayer? (125-126) The answer to this is affirmative among many Christians who have been practicing Zen in Japan and elsewhere for a generation more.

The more recent collection of Stewart and Shaw (1994) contains studies of the transposition of Islam to Sierra Leone, the relationship between Protestant missions and African tribal phenomena and the independent churches, Zionist healing practices among the Zulus, and Roman Catholicism among the Hindus of Tamil Nadu. There is a study of the political effects of syncretistic practices in colonialized Papua New Guinea, another on the nationalist aspects of syncretism in modern Greece, a controversial tribal-festival in Venezuela, syncretism and tradition in Japan, the question of fireworks among Muslims in Germany, and the problem of tolerance and syncretism in India, especially between Hindus and Muslims.

Definitions

This appendix in particular, dealing with "neutral" interpretations of syncretism, points toward the best working definition of the phe-

nomenon. Along the way to a working definition, Walter Capps has
observed that "the process of syncretism is inaccessible apart from
the concrete instances in which it has occurred" (Capps in Pearson,
1975, 44). He argues that one must thus examine a phenomenon
within a definite discipline (anthropology, sociology, history of religions), and not simply in "the phenomenology of religion," in order
to avoid the danger of premature synthesis (42). Granting the importance of this approach, the phenomenological *epoché* should gov-
ern any examination in search of a neutral definition.

Along similar methodological lines, Raimundo Panikkar points out
how syncretism gets investigated after the fact: "In a word, syncretism is a fundamentally factual, often practical, attitude" (Panikkar,
1975, 47-62, at 55). Along with most of the more recent scholars we
have discussed, for Panikkar, syncretism (which he prefers to call
"eclecticism") (50), is ideally a healthy growth toward a *Gestalt*, or a
healthy *eidos* or religious form, in the language of phenomenology.
Helmer Ringgren (1969, 1-14) agrees with this attitude: "One might
say, perhaps, that when a final product becomes functional, it is no
longer syncretism in the narrow sense of the word" (13). Both of
these authors, then, concur with the general thrust of modern studies that "syncretic process" is a more precise way of understanding
the static abstraction "syncretism."

From the perspective of cultural anthropology, Stewart and Shaw
(1994), in an essay that summarizes much of the pertinent scholarship, understand how syncretism, which, simply speaking is just a
religious synthesis, is also a "contentious and contested term which
has undergone many historical transformations in meaning" (1).
Pointing out that it may have many positive characteristics within
culture, the authors state their intention to recast syncretism, as was
done earlier with the concept of "fetishism," into a positive process
of cultural synthesis (2). The term thus has no fixed meaning, but
has been historically constituted and reconstituted, in a process which
the authors call "the politics of religious synthesis" (7), the sub-title
of their book. Within these politics, syncretism can be a process
moving in the direction of authentic "compromise" in order to reach
a healthy synthesis that respects the traditions involved.

The theme of "contest" characterizes the definitional essays of the anthology, *Dialogue and Syncretism* (Gort, 1989). André Droogers begins his essay by carefully reminding readers that there are both the objective and subjective sense of syncretism—that is, the purely descriptive use and the religiously judgmental use (Droogers, in Gort, 1989, 7-25, at 7). Describing the history of the word from Plutarch to Kraemer, he finds Van der Leeuw's concept of "transposition" valuable for interpreting the nature of syncretism: a form's meaning is changed by new cultural and religious interpretations. Naturally, the legitimacy of the alteration depends on the viewpoint of the one witnessing or acknowledging such a transposition. Along with the other authors we have studied, Droogers distinguishes between syncretism as a process and syncretism as a result. He further cautions that we must always inquire as to *what* elements are being mixed—currents of religion, ideology, or other elements—and *how* they are being combined, consciously or unconsciously.

Droogers shares the interest of other authors in the issue of "power" in syncretism—that is, the *political* power to establish criteria among the marginalized or oppressed. The power to decide about authentic or inauthentic syntheses always resides in religious specialists, who also decide what is syncretistic in the negative sense. Those who practice spontaneous and disapproved syncretisms are those without power to change a system, and thus use their own forms of syncretism as protest. Thus, there must be an interpretation of power relationships in such cases, with the hope of achieving a state of social equilibrium and justice. Here Droogers notes the functionalist interpretation such as we have seen discussed above: syncretism serves to overcome ethnic or cultural contradictions. Therefore, functionally speaking, syncretism in a new stage becomes a higher synthesis that guarantees national or group identity in the face of threat.

In a philosophical analysis, Hendrik Vroom (in Gort, 1989, 26-35) chooses a "stipulative definition," or an agreed-upon means of indicating and analyzing the mutual influences between religious traditions. He thus begins by calling syncretism "...the incorporation of incompatible beliefs from one religion by another" (27). This is not the same thing as the condition of contested beliefs, since it is a "logical" rather than a psychological or anthropological category. "The point, however, given the concern here with logic, is the alleged incompatibility of beliefs"—i.e., rather than of practices. Vroom sees any possible dialogue between traditions as grounded in "the existential structure of man" (28), and along with this expresses a hope that all peoples concerned with the problem should have the liberty and opportunity to discuss them. He thus seems to be seeking to raise syncretism from a condition of non-reflexive spontaneity to one of conscious deliberation on compatible and incompatible mixtures.

Seeking more precise understanding of the phenomenon, Vroom goes on to say: "Syncretism is, we can now say, the phenomenon of adopting or wanting to adopt beliefs which are incompatible with beliefs that are logically basic to a belief-system" (33). If the adoption of such truly incompatible beliefs occurs, the original religious configuration of a tradition is essentially altered. Such deep divisions might also arise in ritual matters, depending on the kinds of experiences they evoke. More, while certain incompatibilities figure *within* traditions, they are mediated by a prioritizing of truths, and the incompatibility of syncretism lies in its threat to a central belief system.

Dirk Mulder's concluding summary in the Gort symposium focuses on the issue of "contesting," which depends, of course, on who possesses the power to interpret definitively. Since so many authorities have outright rejected the term "syncretism," Mulder recommends using the word "interpenetration," to describe what occurs prior to any condemnation of it as a syncretism. Observing that theological debates did arise during the symposium, Mulder acknowledges that this is only fitting, given that participants, even in a "descriptive" symposium, do have their own beliefs. Thus, the conversation in the future should proceed not only to deal with "contested interpenetration," but with the question "by whom and for what reason?" (Mulder, 1989, 203-211 at 207)

Mulder's conclusion indicates a preference for the process of interreligious dialogue. He quite wisely rejects the "lowest common denominator" approach, but does advocate agreement on points such as belief in the oneness of humankind, the dignity of persons, the demand for justice, and suggests that the fundamental issues of the existence of God, the meaning of life, and the place of humans in the cosmos continue to be discussed in the light of that agreement.

BIBLIOGRAPHY

Aberle, David. 1982 *The Peyote Religion Among the Navajo Indians*, Chicago: University of Chicago Press.

Ahrens, Theodor 1991 "Zum Synkretismus melanesischer Volkskultur" in Siller, 1991, 62-83.

Alstrom, G.W. 1975 "Heaven and Earth: at Hazar and Adad" in Pearson, 1975, 1-19.

Amaladoss, Michael 1997 *A la rencontre des cultures: comment conjuger unité et pluralité dans les églises?*, Paris: Les Editions Ouvrières.

Anderson, Gerald W. and Stransky, Thomas, J., Ed. 1981 *Mission Trends No.5: Faith Meets Faith*, New York: Paulist; Grand Rapids, MI: William B. Eerdmans

Arrupe, Pedro, 1978 "To the Whole Society," in *Studies in the International Apostolate of Jesuits*, Vol.VII, No.1., June, 1-9.

Bergmann, Jan 1975 "Beitrag zum Interpretatio Graeca: Aegyptische Gotter in Griechischer Ubertragung" in Pearson, 1975.

Berner, Ulrich 1991 "Synkretismus und Inkulturation" in Siller, 1991.

Bevans, Stephen B. 1992 *Models of Contextual Theology*, Maryknoll, NY: Orbis.

Boff, Leonardo 1986 *Church: Charism and Power: Liberation Theology and the Institutional Church*, trans. John W. Dierckesmeier.

Capps, Walter H. 1975 "Uppsala Methodology and the Problem of Religious Syncretism: An Afterward on Prolegomena," in Pearson, 1975.

Carrasco, David 1990 *Religions of Mesoamerica: Cosmovision and Ceremonial Centers*, San Francisco: Harper-Collins.

Collingwood, R.G. 1946 *The Idea of History*, London: Oxford.

Colpe, Carsten 1987 "Syncretism," in Eliade, 1987, 218-227.

Corrington, John William 1979 "Order and Consciousness/Consciousness and History" in McKnight, 1975, 155-195.

Cox, Harvey 1966 *The Secular City: A Celebration of its Liberties and an Invitation to its Discipline*, New York: Macmillan.

Crollius, Ary Roest 1984 *Inculturation: Working Papers on Living Faith and Cultures*, Rome: Editrice Pontifica Universita Gregoriana, Vol. V.

Crowe, Frederick C. 1989 *Appropriating the Lonergan Idea*, Ed. Michael Vertin, Washington, DC: The Catholic University of America Press.

Csikszentmihalyi, Mihaly 1990 *Flow: The Psychology of Optimal Experience*, New York: Harper and Row.

Daniélou, Jean and Marrou, Henri 1964 *The First Six Hundred Years*, in Roger Aubert, ed., *The Christian Centuries*, Vol 1, tr. Vincent Cronin, London: Darton, Longmans and Todd.

Doran, Robert 1990 *Theology and the Dialectics of History*, Toronto: University of Toronto Press.

Dorsey, George A. 1903 *The Arapaho Sun Dance: Ceremony of the Offerings Lodge*, Chicago: Field Columbian Museum 1903a (w. Kroeber, Alfred) *Traditions of the Arapaho*, Chicago: Field Columbian Museum

Douglas, Bruce 1978 "A Diminished Gospel: A Critique of Voegelin's Interpretation of History" in McKnight, 1978, 139-154.

Droogers, André. 1989 "Syncretism: The Problem of Definition, the Definition of the Problem," in Gort et. al., 1989, 7-25.

D'Sa, Francis, S.J. 1991 "Der 'Synkretismus' von Raimundo Panikkar," in Siller, 1991, 130-144

Dunne, John S. 1972 *Way of all the Earth: Experiments in Truth and Religion*, NY: Macmillan

Dupuis, Jacques, S.J. 1997 *Toward a Christian Theology of Religious Pluralism*, Maryknoll, NY: Orbis

Eboussi Boulaga, F. 1977 *La crise du Muntu: authenticité Africaine*, Paris: Presence Africaine

————. 1981 *Christianity Without Fetishes*, trans. Robert R. Barr, Maryknoll, NY: Orbis

Eck, Diana. 1993 *Encountering God: A Spiritual Journey from Bozeman to Banaras*, Boston, Beacon Press

Eliade, Mircea. 1987 *Encyclopedia of Religion*, Vol.14, NY:Macmillan

Elizondo, Vergil. 1997 *Guadalupe: Mother of the New Creation*, Maryknoll, NY: Orbis

Erasmus, Desiderius, 1913 *Opus Epistolarum Des. Erasmi Rotterdami*, eds.P.S. Allen and H.M. Allen, Oxonii: In Typographeo Clarendomano MCMXIII, Tom.III, 1517-1519

Evans, Robert F. 1972 *One and Holy: The Church in Latin Patristic Thought*, London: SPCK

Geertz, Clifford. 1973 *The Interpretation of Cultures*, NY: Basic Books

————. 1995 *After the Fact: Two Countries, Four Decades, One Anthropologist*, Cambridge, MA: Harvard University Press

Gesch, Patrick, S.V.D. 1991 "Der 'Synkretismus' einer Dorfreligion" in Siller, 1991 84-94

Gilson, Etienne. 1955 *The History of Christian Philosophy in the Middle Ages*, New York: Random House

Gort, Jerald et al. eds. 1989 *Dialogue and Syncretism: An Interdisciplinary Approach*, Grand Rapids, MI: William B. Eerdmans

Greverus, Anne Marie. 1991 "Prinzip Collage," in Siller, 1991, 18-30

Guillemette, François. 1995 "L'apparition du concept d' inculturation: une reception de Vatican II," Ottawa:*Mission: Journal of Mission Studies*, Vol.2, No.1 (1995), 53-78

Habermas, Jürgen. 1970 *Toward a Rational Society: Student Protest, Science and Politics*, trans.Jeremy J.Shapiro, Boston: Beacon Press

————. 1971 *Knowledge and Human Interests*, trans. J.J. Shapiro, Boston, Beacon Press

Hanke, Lewis. 1959 *Aristotle and the American Indians: A Study in Race Prejudice in the Modern World*, Chicago: Henry Regnery

————. 1974 *All Mankind is One: A Study of the Disputation between B. de Las Casas and Juan Ginés de Sepulveda in 1550 on the Intellectual and Religious Capacity of the American Indians*, De Kalb, IL: Northern Illinois University Press

Harnack, Adolph. 1904 *The Expansion of Christianity in the First Three Centuries*, trans. James Moffatt, New York: Williams and Norgate, Vol.I 1905 Vol.II.

Hartmann, Sven S. (ed). 1969 *Syncretism: Based on Papers on Cultural Contact, Meeting of Religions and Syncretism held at Åbo on the 8th-10thof Sept. 1966*, Stockholm: Almqvist and Wiksell

Hastings, James (ed). 1922 *Hastings Encyclopedia of Religion and Ethics*, New York: Charles Scribner's Sons, Vol.12

Hilger, Sister Mary Inez. 1952 "Arapaho Child Life and its Cultural Background," *Bureau of American Ethnology Bulletin*, Smithsonian Institution, Washington, DC: United States Government Printing Office, No.148

Hocking, William Ernest et al. 1932 *Rethinking Missions: A Layman's Inquiry after One Hundred Years*, New York: Harper

Hocking, William Ernest. 1940 *Living Religions and a World Faith*, New York: Macmillan

————. 1973 *The Coming World Civilization*, Westport, CT: Greenwood Press (Original, 1956)

Hultkrantz, Åke. 1966 "Pagan and Christian Elements in the Religious Syncretism among the Shoshone Indians of Wyoming," in Hartmann, 1969, 15-40

Jonas, Hans, *The Gnostic Religion: The Message of the Alien God and the Beginnings of Christianity*, (Boston: Beacon Press, 1963)

Jorgensen, Joseph. 1972 *The Sun Dance Religion: Power for the Powerless*, Chicago: University of Chicago Press

Jungmann, Josef. 1959 *The Early Liturgy to the Time of Gregory the Great*, trans. Francis A. Brunner, C.Ss.R., Notre Dame, IN: Univesity of Notre Dame Press

Kapelrud, Arvid S. 1969 "Israel's Prophets and their Confrontation with the Canaanite Religion," in Hartmann, 1969, 162-170

Kraemer, Hendrik. 1961 *The Christian Message in a Non-Christian World*, London: James Clark and Co. Ltd (Original, 1938)

————. 1961 *Religions and the Christian Faith*, New York: Lutterworth Press (Original, 1938)

Kraft, Charles H. 1996 *Anthropology for Christian Witness*, Maryknoll, NY: Orbis

Kroeber, Alfred. 1902 *The Arapaho*, New York: Bulletin of the American Museum of Natural History, Vol.XVIII, Part I

————. 1907 *The Arapaho*, Part II, Religion

La Barre, Weston. 1970 *The Peyote Cult*, New York: Schocken Books

Lanternari, Vittorio. 1963 *The Religions of the Oppressed*, trans. Lisa Sergio, New York: Alfred Knopf

Lévy-Strauss, Claude. 1966 *The Savage Mind*, trans. George Weidenfel, Chicago: University of Chicago Press

Lonergan, Bernard J.F. 1972 *Method in Theology*, New York: Herder and Herder

————. 1992 *Insight: A Study in Human Understanding*, Toronto: University of Toronto Press

Luzebetak, Louis J. 1989 *The Church and Cultures: New Perspectives in Theological Anthropology* (Revised edition) Maryknoll, NY: Orbis

MacMullen, Ramsey. 1997 *Christianity and Paganism in the Fourth to Eighth Centuries*, New Haven and London: Yale Univerity Press

Marsilius of Padua. 1980 *Defensor Pacis*, trans. Alan Gewirth, Toronto: University of Toronto Press

May, John d'Arcy. 1991 "Synkretismus oder Synthese? Eine Antizipatorischen Skizze des religiosen Wandeln im Pazifik," in Siller, 1991

McKnight, Stephen A. ed. 1978 *Eric Voegelin's Search for Order in History*, Baton Rouge: Louisiana State University Press

Meyerhoff, Barbara. 1974 *Peyote Hunt: The Sacred Journey of the Huichol Indians*, Ithaca, NY: Cornell University Press

Moffett, James. 1922 "Syncretism," in Hastings, 1922, 155-157

Möhler, Johann Adam. 1996 *Unity in the Church, or The Principle of Catholicism, Presented in the Spirit of the Church Fathers of the First Three Centuries*, ed. and trans. Peter C. Erb, Washington DC: The Catholic University of America Press

Moltmann, Jürgen. 1977 *The Church in the Power of the Spirit: A Contribution to Messianic Ecclesiology*, trans.Margaret Kohl, London: SCM Press

Mulder, Dirk. 1989 "Dialogue and Syncretism: Some Concluding Observations," in Gort et al., 1989

Niebuhr, H. Richard. 1951 *Christ and Culture*, New York: Harper and Row

———. 1978 *The Responsible Self: An essay in Christian Moral Philosophy*, New York: Harper and Row

Nkeramihigo, Theoneste. 1984 "Inculturation and the Specificity of Christian Faith," in Crollius, 1984, 21-29

Nordland, Odd. 1969 "Valhall and Helgofall: Syncretistic Traits of the Old Norse Religion," in Hartmann, 1969, 68-99

Pagels, Elaine. 1979 *The Gnostic Gospels*, New York: Random House

Panikkar, Raimundo. 1975 "Some Notes on Syncretism and Eclecticism Related to the Growth of Human Consciousness," in Pearson, 1975, 47-62

Pannenberg, Wolfhart. 1971 *Basic Outlines in Theology*, trans.George H. Kehm, London: SCM Press

Paton, W.R., Polenz, M., and Sieveking, W., *Plutarchi Moralia*, 1972 Leipzig: BSB BG Teubner Verlagsgesellschaft

Pearson, Birger A., ed. 1975 *Religious Syncretism in Antiquity: Essays in Conversation with Geo Widengren*, Missoula, MT: Scholars Press

Pelikan, Jaroslav. 1993 *Christianity and Classical Culture: The Metamorphosis of Natural Theology in the Christian Encounter with Hellenism*, New Haven, CT: Yale University Press

Peelman, Achiel. 1988 *L'inculturation: L'Église et les cultures*, Paris and Ottawa: Desclée/Novalis

Perry, John F., S.J. 1998 "Juan Martinez de Ripalda and Karl Rahner's Supernatural Existential," *Theological Studies*, Vol.59, No.3 (Sept), 442-456

Petersson, Olaf. 1969 "Foreign Influences on the Idea of God in African Religions," in Hartmann, 1969, 41-65

Pusey, Michael. 1987 *Jürgen Habermas*, New York: Tavistock Publications and Ellis Horwood, Ltd.

Pye, Michael. 1971 "Syncretism and Ambiguity," *Numen*, Vol.18, 83-93

Quevedo Bosch, Juan. 1996 "El Bembe: The Reveille of the Deities," Toronto: Regis College, Toronto School of Theology, Unpublished Paper

Rahner, Hugo. 1963 *Greek Myths and Christian Mystery*, trans. Brian Battershaw, London: Burns and Oates

Rahner, Karl. 1964 "Visions and Prophecies," *Inquiries*, trans.Charles H. Henkey and Richard Strachan, New York: Herder and Herder, 87-188.

———. 1979 "Toward a Fundamental Theological Interpretation of Vatican II," *Theological Studies*, Vol.40, No.4, December, 716-727

Randall, John Hermann. 1970 *Hellenistic Ways of Deliverance and the Making of the Christian Synthesis*, New York: Columbia University Press

Reilly, Michael Collins. 1978 *Spirituality for Mission*, Maryknoll, NY: Orbis

Ringgren, Holmer. 1969 "The Problem of Syncretism," in Hartmann, 1969, 1-14

Rudolph, Kurt. 1979 "Synkretismus: vom theologischem Scheltwort zum religionswissenschaftlichen Begriff," *Humanitas Religiosa:Festschrift fur Haralds Biezais zu seinem 70. Geburtstag*, Stockholm: Almqvist and Wiksell, 194-212

———. 1983 *Gnosis: the Nature and History of Gnosticism*, trans.Robert MacLachlan Wilson, San Frandisco: Harper and Row

Russell, James C. 1994 *The Germanization of Early Medieval Christianity: A Socio-Historical Approach to Religious Transformation*, New York: Oxford University Press

Sanneh, Lamin. 1993 *Translating the Message: The Missionary Impact on Culture* Maryknoll, NY: Orbis

Scannone, Juan Carlos, S.J. 1991 "Kulturelles Mestizentum, Volkskatholicismus und Synkretismus in Latein Amerika" in Siller, 1991, 106-116

Schineller, J. Peter. 1992 "Inculturation and Syncretism: What is the Real Issue?" *International Bulletin of Missionary Research*, Vol. 16, No.2, 50-53

Schreiter, Robert J. 1985 *Constructing Local Theologies*, Maryknoll, NY: Orbis

———. 1993 "Defining Syncretism: An Interim Report," *International Bulletin of Missionary Research*, Vol.17, No.2, 50-53

———. 1997 *The New Catholicity: Between the Global and the Local Theology*, Maryknoll, NY: Orbis

Segelberg, Eric. 1991 "Old and New Testament Figures in Mandean Version,"in Hartmann, 1969, 228-239

Segundo, Juan Luis. 1976 *The Liberation of Theology*, Maryknoll, NY: Orbis

———. 1984 *Faith and Ideologies*, Maryknoll, NY: Orbis

Shimkin, D.B., "The Wind River Shoshone Sun Dance," *Bureau of American Ethnology Bulletin*, Washington, DC: Smithsonian Institution, United States Government Printing Office, No. 141, pp. 397-484.

Siller, Hermann P. 1991a *Suchbewegungen: Synkretismus - Kulturelle Identität und kirchliches Bekenntnis*, Darmstadt: Wissenschaftliche Buchgesellschaft

———. 1991b "Ein Lernertrag," in Siller, 1991, 193-203

———. 1991c "Synkretismus: Bestandsaufnahme und Problemanzeigen," in Siller, 1991, 1-17

———. 1991d "Synkretistisches Handeln," in Siller, 1991, 174-184

Sjöholm, Gunnar. 1969 "Les limites entre la religion et la culture à l'occasion de l'interprétation de la religion," in Hartmann, 1969, 110-127

Slotkin, James. 1956 *The Peyote Religion: A Study in Indian-White Relations*, New York: Octagon

Song, C.S. 1977 *Christian Mission in Reconstruction*, Maryknoll, NY: Orbis

Starkloff, Carl F. 1992 "Aboriginal Cultures and the Christ," *Theological Studies*, Vol.53, No.2, 288-312

———. 1993 "Attention versus Distraction: Beyond the Quincentennial of Columbus," *Theology Digest*, Vol.40, No.2, Summer, 119- 131

———. 1994a "Inculturation and Cultural Systems," *Theological Studies*, Vol. 55, No.1, March, 66-81; Vol.55, No.2, June, 274-294

————. 1994b "The Problem of Syncretism in the Search for Inculturation," *Mission: Journal of Mission Studies*, (formerly *Kerygma*) Vol.1, No.1, 75-94

————. 1995a "'Good Fences Make Good Neighbors' or 'The Meeting of the Rivers'? Dialogue and Inculturation among Native North Americans," *Studia Missionalia*, Vol.44, 367-388

————. 1995b "In Search of 'Ultimate Meaning' in Arapaho Tradition and Contemporary Experience," *Ultimate Reality and Meaning*, Vol.18, No.4, December, 249-263

————. 1998 "Manitoukaewin: Contemporary Spirituality among Native North Americans," *The Way Supplement*, Vol.91 (1998), 75-87

Steinmetz, Paul B. 1998 *The Sacred Pipe: An Archetypal Theology*, Syracuse: Syracuse University Press

Stendebach, Franz-Josef, O.M.I. 1991 "Zur Frage des Synkretismus im Alten Testament," in Siller, 1991, 31-42

Stewart, Charles, and Shaw, Rosalind (eds.). 1994 *Syncretism/Anti-Syncretism: The Politics of Religious Synthesis*, London and New York: Routledge

Stolzmann, William, S.J. 1986 *The Pipe and Christ: A Sioux-Christian Dialogue*, Chamberlain, SD: St. Joseph's Indian School

Ström, Åke. 1969 "Tradition und Tendenz: Zur Frage des Christliche-vorchristlichen Synkretismus in nordgermanischen Literatur," in Hartmann, 1969, 240-262

Storm, Hyemeyohsts. 1972 *Seven Arrows*, New York: Ballantine Books

Sundermeier, Theo. 1991 "Synkretismus und Religionsgeschichte," in Siller, 1991, 95-105

Tanner, Kathryn. 1997 *Theories of Culture: A New Agenda for Theology*, Minneapolis: Fortress Press

Thomas, M.M. 1974 "Salvation and Humanization: A Discussion" (w. Lesslie Newbigin), in Anderson and Stransky, *Mission Trends No.1*, 217-229

————. 1985 "The Absoluteness of Christ and Christ-Centered Syncretism," *The Ecumenical Review*, Vol.37, 387-397

Thomsen, Harry. 1969 "Non-Buddhist Buddhism and Non-Christian Christianity in Japan," in Hartmann, 1969, 128-136

Tippett, Alan. 1987 *Introduction to Missiology*, Pasadena, CA: William Carey Library

Turner, Victor. 1967 *The Forest of Symbols: Aspects of Ndembu Ritual*, Ithaca, NY: Cornell University Press

————. 1974 *Dramas, Fields and Metaphors: Symbolic Action in Human Society*, Ithaca and London: Cornell University Press

————. 1982 *From Ritual to Theater: The Human Seriousness of Play*, New York: PAJ Publications Cornell University Press

————. 1988 *The Anthropology of Performance*, New York: PAJ Publications Cornell University Press

————. 1995 *The Ritual Process: Structure and Anti-Structure*, New York: Aldine Press (original 1967)

Turner, Victor and Turner, Edith. 1978 *Image and Pilgrimage in Christian Culture: Anthropological Perspectives*, New York: Columbia University Press

Usener, Hermann. 1929 *Götternamen, Versuch einer Lehre von der religiosen Begriffsbildung*, Bonn: Verlag von Friedrich Cohen, Zweiter unveranderte Auflage

Ustorf, Werner. 1991 "Wie über Synkretismus Reden?," in Siller, 1991, 145-149

Van der Leeuw, G. 1963 *Religion in Essence and Manifestation*, trans. J.E. Turner, New York: Harper and Row

Van Dijk, J. 1969 "Les contacts ethniques dans la mesopatomie a les syncretismes de la religion sumerienne," in Hartmann, 1969, 171-206

Van Gennep, Arnold. 1960 *The Rites of Passage*, trans. Monika A. Vizedom, Chicago: University of Chicago Press (Original 1908)

Verkuyl, J. 1978 *Contemporary Missiology: An Introduction*, Grand Rapids, MI: William B. Eerdmans

Visser 't Hooft, W.A. 1963 *No Other Name: The Choice Between Syncretism and Christian Universalism*, London: SCM Press

Voegelin, Eric. 1957. *Order and History*, Baton Rouge, LA: Louisiana State University Press.

———. 1957. *Vol. Two: The World of the Polis*

———. 1957. *Vol. Three: Plato and Aristotle*

———. 1958. *Vol. One: Israel and Revelation*

———. 1974. *Vol. Four: The Ecumenic Age*

———. 1987. *Vol. Five: In Search of Order*

Vroom, Hendrik. 1989 "Syncretism and Dialogue: A Philosophical Analysis" in Gort et. al., 1989

Weiser-All, Lily. 1969 "Syncretism in Nordic Folk Medicine: Critical Periods during Pregnancy," in Hartmann, 1969, 100-109

Werbner, Richard. 1994 "Afterward," in Stewart and Shaw, 1994, 212-215

Widengren, Geo. 1975 "Iran and Israel in Parthian Times with Special Regard to the Ethiopic Book of Enoch," in Pearson, 1975, 85-129

Widenhoffer, Siegfried. 1991 "Methodologische Vor‚berlegungen zur theologischen Synkretismusrede," in Siller, 1991, 150-173

Winter, Gibson. 1968 *Elements for a Social Ethic*, New York: Macmillan

Wiser, James L. 1978 "Philosophy as Inquiry and Persuasion," in McKnight, 1978, 127-138

Zaehner, R.C. 1967 *Mysticism, Sacred and Profane: An Inquiry into Some Varieties of Praeternatural Experience*, London: Oxford University

Zeller, Dieter. 1991 "Die Mysterienkulte und die Paulinische Soteriologie: Eine Fallstudie zum Synkretismus im Neuen Testament," in Siller, 1991, 42-61

INDEX

Abelard, 47
Alfarabi, 47
Albert the Great, 48, 139
Anselm, 44, 46-47, 80, 83, 116, 139
Antelope, 97, 115, 131
anti-structure, 58-59, 172
apartheid, 15
Aquinas, 19, 41, 45-46, 48, 50, 80, 83, 116, 139
Arapaho, 8, 11-12, 93, 96-99, 101-102, 105-106, 111, 113, 117, 130, 167, 169, 172
Avicenna, 47-49

Basil of Caesarea, 30
Bede, 20, 28, 37
Boëthius, 39, 44, 46
Boniface VIII, 14
Bricoleur, 34, 90, 94, 95, 155
bricolage, 5, 94, 126

Calixtus, 144
cargo cult, 75
Carolingian renaisssance, 38
Cassiodorus, 39, 46
common meaning, 84-85, 94, 118, 134
commentary, 111, 130, 133
commentandum, 111, 155
communicative action, 111, 118, 130, 134, 141
communitas, 58-60, 102, 137
compartmentalized dual system, 90
counterposition, 75, 106-108, 128-129
Cretans, 143
culture, 5, 9-10, 12-13, 17, 19, 22, 25-27, 30-35, 38-51, 53, 55, 59-60, 72, 77, 79, 84-85, 89-90, 103-104, 108, 110-111, 116-119, 123, 126, 128, 130, 139, 147, 149-150, 155, 159-160, 162-164, 170-172
culture hero, 117, 128, 163

data of consciousness, 16

Denzinger theology, 76, 82
Debossige, 117
Dewey, 101
direct discourse, 69, 76
disenchantment, 65
Duran, 101

epochs of Christianity, 19, 20
epoché, 63, 119, 127, 157, 164

fetish, 99, 103, 114
Flat Pipe, 93, 98-99
Form, 113
Friday, 11, 93, 95-98, 125, 130
functional specialties, 5, 62, 68, 84, 121, 127
Four Old Men, 12, 96-97

generalized empirical method, 16
Germanization of Christianity, 110
Gestalt, 113, 164
Ghost Dance, 122, 126, 136
gnosticism, 21, 26-27, 30, 35, 55, 80, 111, 160, 171
Grasshopper, 101
Gregory VII, 41
Gregory Nazianzen, 30
Gregory of Nyssa, 30, 35

Handeln, 89, 171
Handlung, 87, 118
heresy, 12, 15, 26, 30, 32, 60, 110-111, 143
heroic culture, 43
horizon, 74
Huichol Indians, 170

in-between, 1, 3, 5-6, 10, 12, 14, 16-22, 24, 26, 28, 30, 32, 34, 36, 38, 40, 42, 44, 46, 48, 50, 52-87, 90, 92, 94, 96, 98, 100, 102, 104, 106, 108, 110, 112, 114, 116, 118, 120, 122, 124, 126-128, 130, 132, 134, 136, 140,

144, 146, 148, 150, 152, 154, 156, 158, 160, 162, 164, 166, 168, 170, 172, 174
inculturation, 10, 12-13, 81, 85, 109, 118, 123, 140, 153, 167-168, 170-172
indirect discourse, 69, 108
internal conversion, 65, 103
Irenaeus, 22-23, 29, 139
Isidore of Seville, 28, 37

Julian, 30-31, 35, 42

koinonia, 54, 148

Las Casas, 32, 36, 49, 168
liminality, 57-60, 62, 103, 126
local theology, 61, 109, 154, 171
logos, 22-24, 28-29, 31-32, 147, 151
Loyola, 62, 133
Luther, 4, 40, 51

Macrina, 30-33, 35
Maimonides, 48
Mana, 112
Medicine Wheel, 93, 113
metaxy, 5, 7, 17-21, 23, 25, 27, 29, 31, 33, 35-37, 39, 41, 43, 45, 47-56, 60, 62, 79, 90, 99-100, 110, 126-127, 139, 141, 154
Minjung theology, 109
Muntu theology, 109

Nazism, 15, 77
Nicholas I, 41
Ndembu, 57, 172

Ockham, 51
Origen, 27-30
Ortiz, 101
Otto I, 41
Ottonian captivity of the Church, 43

participant observation, 127, 134
perspectivism, 73
peyote, 5, 98, 101, 121-129, 131-137, 162, 167, 169-171
peyotism, 98, 101, 121-126

phenomenology, 56, 158, 163-164
pilgrimage, 53, 58-60, 90, 107, 172
pluralism, 9-11, 81, 122, 140, 168
Plutarch, 143, 158, 165
position, 9, 11, 20, 22, 57, 66, 75-76, 106-108, 122, 126, 128, 132, 136-137, 146-147
power as mana, 99, 112, 120
power encounter, 6, 146-148
praxis, 16, 25, 41, 61, 73, 78, 84, 86-87, 89, 95, 101-102, 105, 108, 111, 134, 141
Pueblos, 95

Reformation, 19, 36, 139, 143-144
rites of passage, 57, 102, 173
Redman, 99
reflective conversation, 134
rationalized religion, 65
traditional religion, 65

social drama, 58-59
social strain, 119
sorcery, 114-115, 119-120
structure, 55, 58, 67, 113, 155, 166, 172
Sun Dance, 5, 12, 92-93, 96, 98-99, 101-107, 111, 113, 116, 118, 121, 126, 162-163, 167, 169, 171
Sun Rhodes, 99
Sylvester II, 41
syncretism, 6, 8-18, 21, 23-24, 26, 28, 30-31, 34, 36, 39-45, 47-53, 56, 59-61, 64, 67-69, 71-73, 75-79, 81-82, 84, 86-87, 89-90, 93-94, 102, 105-106, 108-109, 111, 114, 116-117, 122-123, 125, 127, 129, 134, 136, 139-141, 143-173
synthesis, 5, 13, 16, 19, 23-25, 31-32, 36, 39, 41, 45-51, 53, 59, 62, 67, 74, 78-79, 83, 116, 121, 140, 147, 149-150, 159, 164-165, 171-172

Theodoric, 44
Tekakwitha Conference, 91, 95, 99
trickster, 101, 116-117
transposition, 24, 64, 91-93, 95, 157, 163, 165
transcendental precepts, 5, 62, 64, 77

Frank Tyler, 127, 135
Martha Tyler, 135

Vatican Council II, 29, 80

Warren, 101
Will, 113